MW00888211

Ordering Information:
Quantity sales. Special discounts are available on quantity purchases by corporations, associations, and others. For details, contact the publisher at the address above.

Printed in the United States of America

Hall, Jim
Most People Believe In God, Can They All Be Wrong?
The Christianity Counter-Apologetics Handbook /
MSgt Jim Hall USMC (Ret.)

p. cm.

1. Religion — Philosophy. 2. Atheism. — Freethought. 3. Hall, Jim. MSgt (Ret.).

First Edition

14 13 12 11 10 /   10 9 8 7 6 5 4 3 2 1

𝔇edicated to the thinking mammals

of planet Earth who value the
necessity of logic and reason

Introduction

The twentieth and twenty-first centuries have seen developments in mainstream education that are inclusive of pupils with physical disabilities and learning difficulties, even if special services are required in schools to cater for the needs of some pupils.

The same goes for mixtures of skin colours in the same classroom, teaching boys and girls together and treating all nationalities equally.

The fact is that, from a child's first day at school, they mix with children of all abilities and origins and, being children, they are accepting. Bigotry and arbitrary hatred are taught by parents, not developed by the children own their own.

Segregation, then, is a bad thing … but not in one area. Yes, that would be religious segregation. Why parents, and governments, think that it is a "good thing" to segregate children based on which god or gods their parents happen to believe in, so that those children can be indoctrinated to believe in the same god or gods, is a mystery. Or is it?

Religions have fought for centuries to have children indoctrinated in their separate schools and so religious indoctrination in schools is accepted as being the norm because each generation has been subjected to the indoctrination of their own "one true" religion before.

I believe that *all* children should be educated together. When I see classrooms of children of different abilities and, for example, skin colours, I like to think that they are learning about and from each other's' differences. What can possibly be wrong, for the good of the children, for those of different religions to be educated together? Wouldn't the world be a better place if children of all religions, and none, were educated about all religions and none together?

Schools are places of education in facts and reality, different religious and non-religious philosophies should be taught, if necessary at all, away from schools.

Children should be taught **how** to think, not **what** to think.

But how do we impress the importance of educating all children together, equally, without indoctrination, on parents who have already been taught to believe that religious segregation of children is a "good thing"? Well, we discuss the advantages of children of all backgrounds and abilities – and religious or philosophical beliefs – being educated together. And what if a person you are discussing this with is a religionist who believes his or her children should be segregated and indoctrinated? They are convinced that their god or gods is/are the only true god or gods and that their children must be protected from the evils of mixing with children of another go or gods. Now, you will have to start asking why.

When you ask why, you will be met with the absolute truth of the "one true" religion that promotes the "divine words" of the god or gods the person believes in.

Jim Hall has collected together a number of succinct responses to many of the typical arguments posited by religionists. If you are an atheist, you may have come across many of these apologist remarks yourself and been able to provide a rational response. This book, however, manages to not only provide you with more rebuttals than you may already know but also provides invaluable advice on how to discuss matters without being led away from the points you are trying to make.

I commend this book to all those who want to learn how to debate with a religionist and also 'old hands' who want a handy, quick-reference volume to jog their memories when the going gets tough.

I am honoured to have been invited to write this introduction to Jim Hall's excellent guide to tackling religionists' irrational dogma.

I first met Jim in Munich (the one in Germany, not the one in North Dakota). I had travelled there from my home, in Ireland, to visit IBKA's 2012 European Atheist Conference. As a member of Atheist Ireland, I wanted to both support our Chair, Michael Nugent, and also get to see some of the world's other leading atheist speakers.

I met Jim in the hotel bar and we "clicked" straight away. I discovered that he had traveled to the conference from his US Marine Corps base in Germany. Having been in the military myself (the Royal Air Force), I was very interested to hear of Jim's service in the Middle East. I believed then, and I still believe, that Jim frequently put himself in harm's way to protect his own, his family's and all Americans' way of life. Indeed, thousands of atheist Americans – military, policemen and women, firemen and women and paramedics – put themselves in harm's way, on a daily basis, to serve their fellow citizens and country.

Far from being celebrated for their efforts, such atheists are vilified, most notably by then Vice President George H. W. Bush who, on 27th August 1987, said:

"I don't know that atheists should be regarded as citizens, nor should they be regarded as patriotic. This is one nation under God."
(Source: http://www.robsherman.com/advocacy/0604 01a.htm)

The US Constitution requires a Secular government and State. To this day, however, we see the US Military driving a coach and horses through the Constitution it is charged to protect. From Courts Martial refusing to allow evidence from service people who refuse to swear on the Bible, to a West Point cadet being subjected to a pattern of invasive and harassing religious proselytising at the academy, non-religious, patriotic American service men and women are illegally discriminated against.

The USA has a secular Constitution. Ireland does not. All government powers derive "under God"; Judges, the President and members of the Council of State (the Irish President's independent advisory panel) **must** swear a Christian, religious oath to take office and "the homage of public worship is due to Almighty God".

So, the fight to protect US citizens from religious interference with their lives, as provided for under the US Constitution, must continue, whilst, in Ireland, the fight for a secular State, an end to government sanctioned – and financed – religious indoctrination in 93% of Irish schools and equal rights to medical treatment for women, who have no right to choose what they can do with their bodies, is one that must first overcome the undemocratic influence of the Roman Catholic church.

Jim's book will be of use to anyone who debates equal treatment for all with religionists, especially Christians, with their numerous creeds. It offers "old hands" a reminder of some of the arguments they may have forgotten – and maybe some new ones – and it offers newcomers to arguing the common sense and rationality that is atheism very good advice on how to keep control of religionists who veer off the point.

I shall certainly be carrying a copy with me at all times.

Jon Pierson, BSc., LLB. Atheist activist and Campaigner.

Bellewstown
Co. Meath
Ireland

March 2013

Table of Contents

1 Religion does no harm. Why do you have to go after religion? It gives people comfort, it doesn't hurt anything. Pg. 30

2 Why Is There Something Rather Than Nothing? Pg. 36

3 Why not believe in God? Isn't believing the safer bet? Pg. 40

4 You cannot prove that God doesn't exist! Pg. 47

5 Jesus died for our sins. His miraculous birth, death and resurrection is proof of his divinity. Pg. 50

6 We all fall short of the glory of God. We are all born into sin. Pg. 60

7 The universe and life on Earth are so complex, they must have been intelligently designed. Pg. 64

8 Most people believe in God, can they all be wrong? Pg. 73

9 I survived a horrific illness/disease/car wreck, and the only explanation is that it was a miracle. God was watching over me. Pg. 77

10 You don't want to believe in God! You just deny God so you have an excuse to commit sins. Pg. 83

11 God answers my prayers. Pg. 86

12 God speaks to me personally. Pg. 90

13 That was the Old Testament. Those laws don't apply to us anymore. Pg. 94

14 The Bible is the perfect, infallible word of God. Pg. 100

15 You just need to have an open mind. Pg. 105

16 The New Testament is trustworthy in terms of the history it tells us. The Gospels are rooted in eyewitness testimony. Pg. 108

17 Why do you use the Lord's name in vain when you don't even believe in him? Pg. 111

18 If you don't believe in God, you have no moral compass to guide you. What is stopping you from committing crimes? Pg. 116

19 Did you see the big bang with your own eyes? Then you can't know for sure that God didn't create the universe. Pg. 127

20 The universe is finely tuned for life. Strong evidence for a designer comes from the fine-tuning of the universal constants and the solar system. Pg. 130

21 Evolution is only a theory. Pg. 134

22 You are trying to use your atheism and/or material possessions to fill a god-shaped hole in your heart. Pg. 140

23 I will pray for you. Pg. 144

24 What do you tell your children? How do you raise your children? Pg. 147

25 Logical Fallacies Pg. 151

Preface

You're hanging out with friends one evening, and the subject of conversation turns to religion. You are the only atheist in the group and, as the dialogue progresses, all eyes eventually (and predictably) land on you. The self-appointed leader of this impromptu coalition of God-fearing rednecks[1] stands up, takes another long pull off his can of Natural Light, and exclaims "well, you can't prove that God *doesn't* exist!".

Ordinarily, you could debate these guys with one hemisphere of your brain tied behind your back, but this particular question catches you flat-footed. Luckily, you remembered your handy *Christianity Counter-Apologetics Handbook* in your coat pocket. Instead of stumbling through your mental Rolodex to recount the precise rebuttal, you put down your glass of 2006 Fattoria Petrolo Merlot and unleash an intellectual bitch-slapping that all good Christian friends deserve from time to time, leaving them all with their tails between their legs and anxious to change the subject back to football and chicks.

---

[1] I use this as a term of endearment. Living in Texas, most of my friends are rednecks, and proud of it.

The purpose of this book is not to tell my fellow atheists what to think or say when confronted by a theist's arguments. Quite the contrary. Most of the atheists I have ever met are quite capable of defending their lack of belief. Think of this book as just another tool for your toolbox of knowledge. If you find at least one new concept within these pages that sparks your independent thought towards a previously unexplored path of counter-apologetic research, then mission accomplished.

Religious people *can* be logical. That is not to say that *religion itself* must also be logical! All it means is that normally logical people can *also* be irrational with regard to certain facets of their lives. This is a reality to which many Christians aren't willing to admit. You're probably a smart person, dear reader, and capable of thinking critically. Whether you are a person of faith or a non-believer, I urge you to not accept anything in this book without doing some independent research. Think of this handbook simply as a springboard to get you started on, or a catalyst to rekindle, your quest to investigate the veracity of the Christian faith.

If you are a Christian and bought this book to see what "the other side" has to say, I have a suggestion. Put this book down and pick up the Bible. Odds are, you have *never* read it completely. Odds are, the only verses with which you are familiar are the ones your pastor has cherry-picked and fed to you. Odds are, you are unaware of the myriad atrocities, contradictions, absurdities, fallacies of logic, immoralities and unfulfilled prophecies the Bible contains. The first step in studying the truth claims in Christianity *must* be to go to the source, the Bible.

"If you're considering becoming an atheist, read the Bible from cover to cover. No study guides, no spins, just read it. Sometime between when God tells Abraham to kill his son and when Jesus tells everyone to put him before their families, you'll be an atheist."[2]

So, go ahead, put this book on the shelf and *read your Bible*. I'll see you in a month or two.

Oh hey, you're back! How did it go? Shook your pillars of faith a little, right? Ok, *now* that you have started to free yourself of your *delusion*, you are in a position to read this book with its intended purpose in mind!

Delusion [dih-*loo*-zh*uh* n] noun, a *fixed false* belief that is *resistant to reason* or confrontation with actual fact.[3]

---

[2] Penn Jillette, "Penn Jillette's 6 Favorite Books", The Week, 17 Nov. 2012
[3] www.dictionary.reference.com

Quick note: I frequently use "it" in place of the more common "he" when referring to an alleged god. I feel it makes more sense. Unless, of course, the god in question:

1   Exists in the natural universe (implying it is *not* supernatural in origin).
2   ~~Is made of atoms.~~
3   Has a penis. ←Insists God is human

~~Why couldn't~~ God be a woman instead? Perhaps a neutral gender? Multiple gods? Why not a hive-mind consciousness? I've got my money on the Invisible Pink Unicorn[4], which is female.

One more note: I am well aware that I am speaking directly to theists is some sections of this book and fellow infidels in others. I apologize if it seems as though I'm all over the map because of this, but that's just what the flow of information dictated.

As in any aspect of life, it pays to be prepared. Christians *can't stand* a calm, soft spoken, confident, articulate and well-informed atheist. Below are a few tips to keep in mind when, let's say, you are confronted at your doorstep by two starry-eyed boys in white, short-sleeved dress shirts and black ties.

1   Only argue with people who are willing to answer your questions. Having a debate with a close-minded Christian who is not the least bit receptive to, or refuses to acknowledge, any of

---

[4] http://en.wikipedia.org/wiki/Invisible_Pink_Unicorn

the points you are trying to get across is "like masturbating with a cheese grater, slightly enjoyable, but mostly painful".[5] Additionally, I have encountered many of the faithful who refuse to answer any hypothetical questions. This puzzles me, probably because we atheists are so fond of this type of thought experiment. Ask a Christian "if irrefutable proof became available that the god of the Bible does not exist, would you renounce your faith?". I have yet to meet one who can answer that honestly and convincingly. On the flip side, if an atheist is asked what he would do if an acceptable level of evidence for the existence of Yahweh was obtained, chances are he would be willing and able to approach the question honestly.

2   Read books *not* written by atheists. If you limit your reading list only to the likes of Epicurus, Bertrand Russell, Carl Sagan, Richard Dawkins and Bart Ehrman, you will be at a severe disadvantage. If you're like me, you'd almost rather suck on the business-end of a .12 gauge than crack open a book by William Lane Craig, Josh McDowell, Lee Strobel or C.S. Lewis. Do yourself a favor, though, and give it a try. Try to contain your laughter and heed my words: Don't drink coffee while reading these... it will come out through your nose without warning!

---

[5] "The Adventures of Ford Fairlane" (1990)

3   Avoid ad hominem[6] attacks and try not to make fun of believers. However, their beliefs themselves are fair game in my opinion. This is an important distinction. Young-Earth creationists, geocentrists, faith healers, et al, have crazy, outlandish, fantastical and completely ridicule-worthy claims, but the finesse lies in wording your mockery to only attack the idea itself, not the person. That is hypocritical for me to say, as I have often caught myself, for instance, making fun of John Morris Pendleton's ill-fitting lab coat instead of concentrating on his argument that all dinosaurs were herbivores, or using Kent Hovind's fake degree and prison sentence for tax evasion as reasons to discredit his belief that anyone that believes the Earth is over 10,000 years old is possessed by Satan.

4   Choose your battles. Recently, I was at a restaurant with my wife's side of the family to celebrate my daughter's birthday. At one point, I was telling my sister-in-law about the zoo to which we had taken Chloe earlier that day. As I was describing the ape enclosures, my other

[6] Latin for "against the man". Examples include discrediting everything a person says about abortion for no other reason than he is a pastor, or refusing to listen to a person's well thought-out argument against gun control simply because she is a service member in the Armed Forces. Often confused with an outright insult.

daughter Mallory asked what the difference is between an ape and a monkey. I explained that monkeys have tails, and apes such as gorillas, chimpanzees and humans do not. My mother-in-law, visibly shaken by this statement, retorted "well, my daddy used to say that our ancestors didn't swing from their *tails*, but they *did* swing from their *necks* for horse thievery!" There are five reasons I chose not to pursue this debate:

- It was Chloe's birthday. She was about to open gifts and have cake served.

- As I am not an evolutionary biologist, I like to have www.talkorigins.org at my fingertips when I discuss evolution with a creationist. Reading from a smartphone in a loud restaurant just doesn't cut it for me.

- I have been down this path to nowhere with my mother-in-law before. She is too firmly indoctrinated to accept *anything* I have to say on this subject, making it a futile effort.

- My wife, who was sitting next me, is under the impression (correctly, as it turns out) that I am slightly obsessed with debating, especially during the research phase for this book. I really didn't want to see her roll her eyeballs and shoot laser-daggers at me.

- Aria and I have chosen to keep the kids as free from religious (and non-religious) influence as possible. They aren't being raised in a bubble however. Chloe goes to church with her granny,

Mallory often asks me questions about religion, they both have contributed illustrations for this book, and they are getting a well-rounded education in world religions. When they finally reach the age of reason, though, I want them to be in a position to be able to make up their *own* minds about religion (or lack thereof).

5   Agree *beforehand* on what will be debated. If the discussion is open-ended, your opponent will attempt to steer the rudder towards safer waters as soon and she feels that she is losing the argument.

6   Do your homework. Though it's entirely possible to remain on the offensive and entirely from your own perspective, it is the mark of a skilled debater to be equally at ease allowing the opposition venture into your waters. Doing some research ahead of time by studying the pertinent Biblical history, quotes and translation of key words from the original Hebrew or Greek can prove to be invaluable. Any time you think you have a good point, look it up (time permitting of course) to see what has already been said about the topic and modify/scrap the idea in light of the additional information.

7   Be careful when discussing the concept of faith. Yes, it is a target-rich environment, easily picked apart, worthy of ridicule, flawed and

completely illogical. Remember though, you are talking to an individual who has possibly spent a great deal of his life holding on to the delusion that faith is the most important thing in his life. To challenge the bedrock of his entire worldview, especially early in the conversation, is to possibly cause him to put up his psychological defenses with regard to any follow-on topics. In other words, attacking a person's faith usually feels, to the Christian, like a personal attack. No matter how well thought-out and convincing your argument is, *no one* likes to be told that, for instance, their post-graduate degree in theology and their 30 years as a pastor has amounted to absolutely nil. Instead, try to limit your critique of faith to the bigger picture: The church's views on faith, all the horrible wars fought in the name of faith, the fact that faith in the infallibility of the Bible was one of the catalysts for slavery in the United States, or the efficaciousness of faith when tested in controlled laboratory settings.

8   Make it clear from the outset that Christians don't have a monopoly on morality. If you're having a conversation with someone who thinks this, it wouldn't hurt to inform her of the unique facets of your own life which prove that it's possible to be a good person without being a Christian. She may be your best friend in the world but until you put a kind, *moral,* human

face on atheism, there is a very real possibility that she is looking at you right now in pity and thinking that the powers of darkness have inexorably dug their talons into you. A good counter is to point out the disproportionate amount of hypocrisy, perversion and corruption that occurs on a daily basis within the church itself.[7] When asked why Christian values didn't prevent these acts, your debater may seek refuge in the the "free will" defense, that even devout churchgoers and church leaders are free to choose whether or not to be moral. This would be an ideal time to point out that atheists are free to make the same choice, thereby making *Christian* morality completely unnecessary.

9 Jump on flawed logic as soon as you hear it. Perhaps your debater accepts a literal interpretation of the Bible. In that case, it would be wise to have a few biblical self-contradictions (there are *hundreds*) ready and ask which of the verses you are to accept. Additionally, don't forget to point out all the variations in the biblical translations and editing

---

[7] As I was writing this section, I thought I'd test my claim by performing a quick web search using today's date to see how many church leaders were arrested for immoral acts. There were too many to count. The first hit was Louis Joseph Bristol, 28, a Carpinteria California Youth Pastor arrested *four hours ago* on charges of child molestation, child rape, lewd acts upon a child, and furnishing controlled substances to minors.

over time. If you are discussing key concepts in the New Testament and neither of you are able to read Koine Greek, you may consider bringing more that one version of the Bible to the table. The New American Standard Bible (NASB) is considered to be the strict literal interpretation, followed by the King James Version (KJV), New King James Version (NKJV), New International Version (NIV) and New Living Translation (NLT), in descending order of accuracy but ascending ease of reading. If your debater wishes to attempt to reconcile the Bible and scientific facts, point out that faith, *by definition*, is independent of fact and that the need to obtain "evidence" is antithetical to the concept of faith itself. If your debater believes that Jesus is the only way to salvation, ask what her guess is as to the fate of both the Jewish Holocaust victims and Catholic Nazis.

10 Be ready to defend your claims. If you propose, for example, that the scientific method is superior to religious faith, be prepared to counter the inevitable argument that science is in a constant state of change. Even established facts are subject to revision or complete annihilation with the the advent of new discoveries and methods. It is safe to assume that much of what we take for granted today will become defunct in the future. Your

opponent, at this juncture, could be made aware that the dynamic nature of science is precisely what makes it superior to religion! Stephen Hawking: "There is a fundamental difference between religion, which is based on authority, [and] science, which is based on observation and reason. Science will win because it works."[8]

11 Don't expect to de-convert anybody. The freedom of (and from) religion is much more important, in my opinion, than the desire to see our species once and for all unshackled from superstitions. Let go of that need to emerge from the debate victorious. Remember that your opponent can, at any time, claim a draw just by appealing to personal anecdotal evidence or by saying "well, I have faith" and walking out of the room. From my experience, however, the atheist's argument tends to have a long fuse. I have inadvertently planted the seed of doubt in many of my friends and colleagues, only to see it bloom months or even years later.

12 I can almost guarantee that your opponent, be it a close friend or even a family member, will feel the need to raise her voice and become

[8] "Stephen Hawking on Religion: 'Science Will Win'", ABC World News With Diane Sawyer (7 June 2010)

somewhat aggressive at some point in the conversation. Don't follow suit, it will deteriorate into an unproductive shouting match. Your arguments pack much more of a punch when you remain calm. She is simply parroting what she sees her priest or pastor doing every Sunday morning. She will walk into that quicksand on her own, there's no need for you to follow her.

13 *Don't let them start preaching*. They love to let the conversation slip into a one-way sermon. They just can't help it. Keeping them on point is sometimes like washing a cat. This is a tactic designed to change the subject when they feel painted into a corner, and it gives them an air of authority. Once an apologist feels dominant, get ready for contempt, false modesty, condescension and even more preaching. Don't be afraid of hurting their feelings, hold their feet to the fire and *demand* that the conversation not turn into a sermon.

14 I saved the most important tip for last. *Agree on definitions*. There is absolutely no sense in debating at all if the two of you have completely different definitions of the key points, words, terms and phrases. Atheists use logic and reason, so insisting on the agreement of terms should come naturally; however, those of faith (especially the clergy) customarily *hate*

being called upon to to explain their idealess language. They tend to stutter and stagger if you ask one of them to define the word "god" for instance. "If he does not fly into a passion deem yourself fortunate, but as to an intelligible definition, look for nothing of the sort. He can't furnish such definition however disposed to do so."[9] For instance, if someone asks me a seemingly innocuous question like "do you believe in God?", usually the first things out of my mouth are "Which god? Can you define god for me? Define 'belief'. Do you want to know if I accept the existence of a god without any evidence? Are you using the word 'believe' to mean something synonymous to 'guessing', 'hoping' or 'knowing'? Although this really makes you seem like a total dick, it's important to nail down exactly what they are asking. The following is a list of the words that, from my experience, are difficult for theists and infidels to agree upon. It is not an authoritative list, simply the subjective interpretations of your humble author:

Presupposition. To assume a conclusion to be true based on two or more premises. For example, Premise 1: All mammals are warm-blooded. Premise 2: Giraffes are mammals. Conclusion: Giraffes are warm-blooded. In a valid deductive argument, the

---

[9] Charles Southwell, "An Apology for Atheism Addressed to Religious Investigators of Every Denomination"

presupposition is only valid is the premises are true. Now here's a really bad example: Premise 1: The existence of objective morality is not possible without the presence of a divine lawgiver. Premise 2: Humans obviously have an objective morality. Conclusion: The Christian God exists.

Dispensation. An arbitrary, unsupported, unverified claim that the Bible is divided into between four and seven time periods, depending on who you ask. Yahweh allegedly deals with humans differently according to each time period. This is a blatant attempt to justify Yahweh's wishy-washy, unpredictable temperament towards people throughout the ages.

Belief/Faith. Confidence in the truth or existence of something in the absence of any evidence. The most maleficent, contemptible and unfortunate of *all* human qualities.

God. A psychological construct, invented by homo sapiens as soon as they became aware of their own mortality, to feel comfort in the face of death, darkness and the unknown. Keep this in mind: The friend with whom you are debating may or may not believe in a *trinitarian*[10] deity. Does he have a

---

[10] A monotheism, but the deity is composed of three independent parts or aspects. The three are one, but they are also separate. Ask 20 Christians to explain this and you will get 20 different answers. "Sister Joan, what sorts of gifts can we receive from

pantheistic[11] view of his deity? Is it an omnipotent, omnibenevolent and omniscient god?[12] Is it a god of mercy *and* perfect justice?[13] There are many things to consider that make a big difference in a debate.

Bible. A collection of 66 to 81[14] fairy tales written by at least 40 authors, *none* of which *ever* met Jesus, from Asia, Europe and Africa using three different languages over a 1600-year time frame. Literal Interpretation? Book of allegories only?

Jesus. According to myth:
- Born in Bethlehem, to conform to Old Testament Prophecy. His parents traveled there to be present for a Roman census in 6 C.E. However, there is no record, outside the Bible, of the existence of such a census, and it was never a practice in the Roman

---

the Holy Ghost?" Well Suzie, the Holy Ghost usually gives us the gift of a chronic fucking headache trying to rationally explain our horseshit dogma of the trinity".

[11] The belief that "God" is simply the forces of nature and laws of the universe.

[12] I would be remiss if I did not include the *Epicurean Paradox* here: Is God willing to prevent evil, but not able? Then he is not omnipotent. Is he able, but not willing? Then he is malevolent. Is he both able and willing? Then whence cometh evil? Is he neither able nor willing? Then why call him God?

[13] If so, your friend has a dilemma on his hands. If it Yahweh dispenses perfect justice, it would be incapable (or unwilling) to *ever* be merciful.

[14] Depending on who you ask. The number of books in the Bible range from the standard mainstream Protestant (66) to the Ethiopian Orthodox Church (81).

Empire to require people to return to their home city for a census.

- A man from Nazareth, a town that wasn't built until after he died.[15]

- Descendant of King David, although the biblical genealogies vary widely.[16] It is a moot point, though, since Joseph was not Yeshua's biological father.

- There is *no* physical evidence (none, zero, nil, naught, nothing) that supports the historical Jesus. All stories about Yeshua are hearsay upon hearsay, from copies of copies of copies of copies of copies (you get the idea) of manuscripts that were written decades to centuries after his supposed death and resurrection.

- There are *no* extra biblical records that say Pontius Pilate executed anyone named Jesus.

- *None* of the Bible's authors ever actually met Yeshua. Paul was at least 40 years too late and the anonymous gospel writers, affluent Greeks, were almost a century too late.

- In that case, maybe he was just a Prophet, or wise teacher? Sorry, no. The preacher John Duncan (1859) said it best: "Christ either deceived mankind by conscious fraud, or he was himself deluded and self-deceived, or he was divine. There is no getting out of this trilemma. It is inexorable."

---

[15] The Old Testament never mentions Nazareth. In all 13 Epistles, Paul never mentioned it. All Rabbinic texts, including the Talmud which names 63 Galilean towns, says nothing about Nazareth. Things that make you go Hmmm.

[16] Matt. 1:2-17; Luke 3:23-38

Religion does no harm. Why do you have to go after religion? It gives people comfort, it doesn't hurt anything.

- You know what would give *me* great comfort? If the world were free of pedophiles, torture, murder, deadly diseases and natural disasters. Unfortunately, that's not the case. Grow up! *Wishing* for a heavenly afterlife doesn't make it so.

- It doesn't *hurt* anything? Let's see, trying to bring creation pseudoscience into my kids' classrooms, officially turning a blind eye to the Holocaust as it was happening[17], corruption, bombing abortion clinics and murdering its doctors, hypocrisy, hateful intolerance of any opposing viewpoint, anti-science attitude which retards human progress, the devastation caused by AIDS because of a refusal to allow condoms, the silly notion of vicarious redemption[18], the selling of *indulgences*[19] and actually believing faith is a noble human virtue.

---

[17] Additionally, the Vatican regularly sent Adolf Hitler formal birthday greetings! (John Cornwell, "Hitler's Pope: The Secret History of Pius XII")

[18] The repulsive and illogical notion that an animal (in the case of the Old Testament) or another person (in the case of the New Testament) can be substituted to pay for the iniquities of the guilty party or parties. Commonly referred to as *scapegoating*.

[19] Basically, a *get out jail free* card. A cheap method the Catholic Church used for extracting enormous wealth, sinners could simply pay their way to absolution. Dominican Johann Tetzel (1465-1519) was an important promoter of indulgences and was known for the slogan "as soon as the coin in the coffer rings, the soul from purgatory springs."

"Ok, other than most wars, the Crusades, the Inquisition, 9/11, arranged marriages to minors, blowing up schools[20], the suppression of women and homosexuals, fatwas, ethnic cleansing, honor rape, human sacrifice, burning witches, suicide bombings, condoning slavery and the systematic fucking of children. There are a few little things I have a problem with."[21]

- I must admit, the dogmatic assertions of believers, usually mixed with a smug *schadenfreude*[22], is infuriating beyond measure. They wear faith on their chest as a badge of honor, as if it were actually a noble human virtue. When I hear "I will pray for you", it always comes out as a veiled threat.

"Nothing proves the man-made character of religion as obviously as the sick mind that designed hell, unless it is the sorely limited mind that has failed to describe heaven—except as a place of either worldly comfort, eternal tedium, or (as Tertullian thought) *continual relish in the torture of others*[23]."

- Christianity, like most other religions, devalues human life. We send our young warfighters into

---

[20] (And churches, Buddhist statues, office buildings, synagogues and mosques)
[21] Bill Maher, "But I'm Not Wrong" 2010
[22] Pleasure derived from the misfortunes of others
[23] Christopher Hitchens, "God Is Not Great"

battle with the notion that it is OK to die, because once you're dead, you get to go to Heaven, an obvious product of wishful thinking.

- Practicing Christians who hold positions of authority within the government have been, are, and will continue to be dangerous. From local politics to the U.S. presidency. Recently, the Texas Board of Education approved a social studies curriculum which, in effect, rewrites history.[24] For starters, Thomas ("separation between church and state") Jefferson was cut from the list of inspirational revolutionaries. With whom was he replaced? St. Thomas Aquinas and John Calvin. The new textbook also includes displaying Republican philosophies in a more positive light, playing up the superiority of American capitalism and denying that the Founding Fathers' were committed to a secular government.

- According to a recent poll, 41% of all Americans believe Jesus will return in the next 40 years[25] to usher in the apocalypse. Even Jesus allegedly taught that ideas like saving and planning for the future were meaningless, because his second coming is imminent:

---

[24] "Texas Conservatives Win Curriculum Change", New York Times, 12 march 2010

[25] Pew Research Center, July 2010. (Additionally, a full 60% believe Jesus will return *sometime* in the future.)

1   "Do not store up for yourselves treasures on earth, where moth and rust destroy, and where thieves break in and steal. But lay up for yourselves treasures in heaven, where neither moth nor rust doth corrupt, and where thieves do not break through nor steal." (Matt. 6:19,20)

2   "And why do you worry about clothes? See how the lilies of the field grow. They do not labor or spin. Yet I tell you that not even Solomon in all his splendor was dressed like one of these. If that is how God clothes the grass of the field, which is here today and tomorrow is thrown into the fire, will he not much more clothe you, O you of little faith? So do not worry, saying, 'What shall we eat?' or 'What shall we drink?' or 'What shall we wear?'" (Matt. 6:28-31)

3   "So then, you cannot be my disciple unless you give away everything you own." (Luke 14:33)

4   "Look at the birds of the air; they do not sow or reap or store away in barns, and yet your heavenly Father feeds them. Are you not much more valuable than they? Who of you by worrying can add a single hour to his life?" (Matt. 6:26,27)

5   "Therefore do not worry about tomorrow, for tomorrow will worry about itself. Each day has enough trouble of its own." (Matt. 6:34)

- Delusions like those above greatly affect peoples' ideas on the future of our species. It is precisely this type of dark ages nonsense that continues to retard human progress. Don't plan for the future, don't save your money, Don't worry about the environment and, if you see a colossal mushroom cloud in the sky one day, cheer up and take heart, you will be called home soon! Christian irrationality hurts *everyone*.

- On 25 March 2009 at the U.S. House of representatives Subcommittee on Energy and the Environment, Rep. John Shimkus, stated that climate change isn't something to worry about because *God promised he wouldn't destroy the Earth after Noah's flood*. Later, A blogger from Salon, Andrew Leonard, had this to say: "I'm glad that John Shimkus can sleep at night, faithful that God's word is 'infallible, unchanging, perfect.' But for those of us who are less confident in humanity's ability to keep from massively screwing up, the thought that the Bible will be determining government energy policy is massively ulcer inducing."

Why Is There Something Rather Than Nothing?

- I don't know. And *neither do you*!

- This the *cosmological argument*.

- This is an *argument from ignorance*.

- Are you implying there must be a *first cause* or an unmoved mover?

This leads to the problem of *infinite regress*. If something cannot come from nothing, and a god is something, *what created the god*?

- The existence of the universe cannot possibly be used as evidence to support the proposition that god exists.

- The idea of an *uncaused cause* is just answering a mystery with a bigger mystery.

- This question invariably leads to the *fine-tuning argument*, which goes something like this: The universe has a number of dimensionless constants, to include the relative strengths of the four fundamental forces of nature: Gravity, electromagnetism, and the strong and weak nuclear forces. If these values were to have been even minutely different, the universe as we know it would not exist and life would have not been possible.

- If there were a god, why did it wait 13.7 billion years and create more planets than there are grains of sand on all the beaches of Earth, just to make humans in its image on *only one* planet?

- Scientists theorize that given the infinite nature of time and space, an infinite number of other unobservable universes could exist parallel to our own, each with infinite variations of constants. This is known as the *multiverse theory.* Given infinite possibilities, the formation of a universe such as our own is not so inconceivable. If somebody claims to be psychic and they win the lottery three times in a row. That seems to be good evidence. However, if they bought every possible combination of numbers for each of those lotteries. That feat requires no psychic abilities at all. The fine-tuning argument is actually therefore a great argument for atheism. Which theists are wrongly claiming as evidence for God.[26]

- If you are trying to define your god as metaphysically necessary, I'm sorry but you cannot simply *define* something into existence!

---

[26] Iron Chariots Wiki, http://wiki.ironchariots.org/index.php?title=Fine-tuning_argument

- This is actually a question for *science*, not philosophy or theology. Lawrence M. Krauss, a leading theoretical physicist, says "quantum mechanics, combined with the Theory of Relativity, allows *something to come from nothing*! In fact, *'nothing'* is an unstable state of existence!"[27]. Other great quips from Krauss are "God is redundant" and "Forget *Jesus*, the *stars* died so that you could be here today".

- Other possible explanations are Alternative Biochemistry, Bubble Universe Theory,[28] Top-Down Cosmology and Alien Design.

- A made-up answer is *not* better than no answer at all. All Christians do is push this issue back one step, claim victory in the absence of a competing theory, and hope no one looks behind the curtain.

---

[27] "A Universe from Nothing: Why There is Something Rather than Nothing"

[28] Victor Stenger, "The Universe: The Ultimate Free Lunch", European Journal of Physics (1990)

Why not believe in God? Isn't believing the safer bet?

- This is known as *Pascal's Wager*. Now over a century old, it is a common question asked by theists. This boat has so many holes in it, I'm surprised it's still afloat. The premise is basically this: If you believe in God and you're right, you gain eternal salvation and if you're wrong, you've lost nothing. If you deny God and are right, you haven't gained anything but if you are wrong... wailing and gnashing of teeth in a lake of boiling excrement until the end of time awaits you.

- Which God? You are assuming that there's only one religion, and only one version of God. There are hundreds upon hundreds of different religions, and different gods these religions believe in. There currently exist hundreds of actively practiced religions on Earth. Just to be on the conservative side, let's just take the 22 most popular faiths, from Christianity (2.1 billion followers) to Scientology (500 thousand followers). Blaise Pascal, we assume, was referring to Roman Catholicism as the only option. Throw all of the popular religions in the mix, however, and the most devout, pious believer's chances of being right fall to 1:22. Incidentally, although "Secular/Nonreligious/Agnostic/Atheist" is not a religion, it comes in third on the list (1.1 billion people). Many studies show nonbelievers as the fastest growing group, with the Church of

Jesus Christ of Latter Day Saints (Mormonism) coming in a close second.

- How do you know which one to wager on?

- How is it possible to simply *begin* believing? How strong is a person's faith if they only believe in a god to hedge their bets? Do you *really* believe it, or are you trying to fool yourself, or your god, or both? Do you think that, if your god *does* exist, it would be able to see through your charade?

- Is an omniscient god *really* going to be fooled by Pascal's Wager?

- If you obey the rules of one religion, you're guaranteed to be violating the rules of another.

- Christian: Believe in Jesus or burn in hell[29]. Muslim: Believe in Allah or else, and if you believe Jesus was divine it's into the pit for you[30] . For the sake of argument, assume these are your only two options. The chance of you burning in hell is still a coin flip.

- What if *you're* wrong?

---

[29] John 3:36
[30] Sura 5:75; 9:30

- What if God rewards only those who use logic and the reasoning brain that it gave them? In which case, what if only atheists, agnostics, humanists, secularists and freethinkers go to Heaven?

- You are assuming that your god cares whether you believe in it. It assumes that the god you chose will reward belief with a heavenly eternal afterlife, and punish disbelief with a hellish one.

- The *Atheist Wager*:

If God is good, it won't care if you believe in him, just try to be the best person you can be, based on your own understanding.

If God is egoistic, capricious and insecure, then we have no way of knowing what behavior it's going to punish or reward, and we might as well just be good according to our own understanding.

If there is no god, then it's worth being good for its own sake. We should therefore have compassion for other people, because being good makes our world a better place, for ourselves and everyone else.

[handwritten margin note: The definition of good cannot be established from human ideas and ... to say that we are good as we understand it is saying that we to are to do as our minds perceive it]

- It isn't an argument. It's an excuse for why you don't have an argument. And it's a completely pathetic excuse.

- Is your god *that* gullible, or just *dumb*? To buy into Pascal's Wager, you have to first accept the following: 1. God requires that you believe in him; 2. The god you chose to believe in actually exists; 3. He is easily fooled.

- Are you able to just choose what you want to believe, like choosing which cereal you want for breakfast? If this wager is the primary motive for your belief, you are not just trying to fool your god, you're trying to fool yourself. Either your belief is not sincere and God will know it, or you have no concept of the definition of the word "belief".

- You seem to think that "believing" means "professing an allegiance to an opinion, regardless of whether you think it's true." To paraphrase Inigo Montoya: You keep using that word "believe." I do not think it means what you think it means.

Christianity: The belief that an invisible Jewish lich will grant you immortality if you eat his flesh, drink his blood and telepathically tell him that you accept him as your master, so he can wash away all the evil forces that have invaded your soul because one of your great-great grandmothers was tricked by a talking

45

snake to eat from a magical tree. The lich loves you, but he has prepared a lake of eternally-boiling sulfur for you just in case you don't love him back.

You cannot prove that God *doesn't*

exist!

- You're correct. I also cannot prove that Santa Claus, leprechauns, invisible pink unicorns, the flying spaghetti monster, vampires or jackalopes don't exist either. Does *that* make them real?

- The burden of proof is on the one who *makes* the assumption. The person that makes a claim must demonstrate the truth of that claim, or at the very least, provide a single piece of testable, verifiable evidence.

- The ever-improving scientific claims on the nature of the universe are infinitely more compelling than a book of fairy tales written by semi-literate nomadic iron age desert goat herders.

- "What can be asserted without evidence can also be dismissed without evidence."[31]

- I don't claim to know for sure that gods don't exist; however, you *don't* get to claim victory by default.

---

[31] Christopher Hitchens

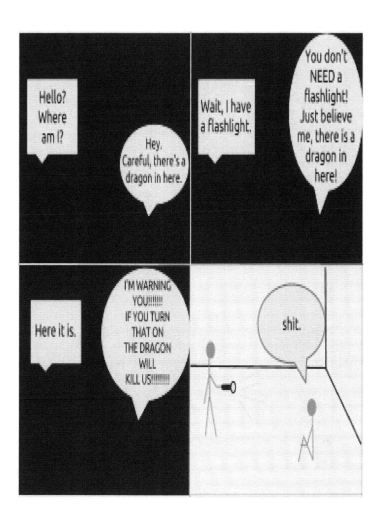

Jesus died for our sins. His miraculous birth, death and resurrection is proof of his divinity.

- Jesus' body was interred by Joseph of Arimathea. After sundown, some of his followers (not the disciples) visited his tomb, reverently removed his body, and buried him in a secret location. Is this scenario likely? Not really. Is this is what *really* happened? Probably not. Is this scenario *more* probable than a supposed *miracle* of divine resurrection and ascension to heaven? Yes, and here's why: By definition, a *highly unlikely* event is far more probable than a *miracle*. Hence the word "miracle".

- There is no good reason to believe Joseph of Arimathea allowed Jesus' body to be placed in his tomb, or that the Romans would have allowed it.

- Any number of scenarios could be created to explain the empty tomb and would not require the absurd notion that Yahweh did it.

- It is important to emphasize that the "honorable burial" and "empty tomb" are not facts at all, and not even mentioned by Paul. Rather, it is later embellishment created by Mark, at least 30 years after Jesus' death. The book of John was written as late as 115 CE. All the gospels were written in *Greek*, not in Aramaic, by *anonymous* authors. The names ascribed to the authors were arbitrarily added much later.

- The predicted Messiah[32] was supposed to be a *warrior*, come to deliver the Jews out of Roman rule. It goes without saying that the crucifixion of the man many of the Jews thought was their liberator came as quite a disappointment. Essentially, the Christ figure rose out of that disappointment. Started by Paul, who self-admits he never met the guy. Others, in later decades, anonymous writers who didn't live in Judea nor Galilee, had never been there, didn't know the language - wrote the Gospel stories we now know, while sitting in another country, writing in another language.

- According to the Bible, *Jesus wasn't the only one who was resurrected*:

1 Then said the woman, Whom shall I bring up unto thee? And he said, Bring me up Samuel ... And he said unto her, What form is he of? And she said, *An old man cometh up*; and he is covered with a mantle. And Saul perceived that it was Samuel. [33]

2 And the LORD heard the voice of Elijah; and the soul of the child came into him again, *and he revived*.[34]

---

[32] Who incidentally was predicted to be named *Emmanuel*, not Jesus.

[33] 1 Sam. 28:11, 14

[34] 1 Kings 17:22

3   And when Elisha was come into the house, behold, the child was dead, and laid upon his bed. He went in therefore, and shut the door upon them twain, and prayed unto the LORD. And he went up, and lay upon the child, and put his mouth upon his mouth, and his eyes upon his eyes, and his hands upon his hands: and stretched himself upon the child; and the flesh of the child waxed warm. Then he returned, and walked in the house to and fro; and went up, and stretched himself upon him: *and the child sneezed seven times.*[35]

4   And it came to pass, as they were burying a man, that, behold, they spied a band of men; and they cast the man into the sepulchre of Elisha: and when the man was let down, and touched the bones of Elisha, *he revived, and stood up on his feet.*[36]

5   And when Jesus came into the ruler's house, and saw the minstrels and the people making a noise, He said unto them, Give place: for the maid is not dead, but sleepeth. And they laughed him to scorn. But when the people were put forth, he went in, and took her by the hand, *and the maid arose.*[37]

6   And the graves were opened; *and many bodies of the saints which slept arose, and came out*

---

[35] 2 Kings 4:32-35
[36] 2 Kings 13:21
[37] Matt. 9:23-25

of the graves after his resurrection, and went into the holy city, and appeared unto many.[38]

7   Now when he came nigh to the gate of the city, behold, there was a dead man carried out, the only son of his mother, and she was a widow: and much people of the city was with her. And when the Lord saw her, he had compassion on her, and said unto her, Weep not. And he came and touched the bier: and they that bare him stood still. And he said, Young man, I say unto thee, Arise. *And he that was dead sat up, and began to speak*. And he delivered him to his mother.[39]

8   And when he thus had spoken, he cried with a loud voice, *Lazarus, come forth*.[40]

- "Now the birth of Jesus Christ was in this wise. When his mother, Mary, was espoused to Joseph, before they came together she was found with child of the Holy Ghost. Yes, and the Greek demigod Perseus was born when the god Jupiter visited the virgin Danae as a shower of gold and got her with child. The god Buddha was born through an opening in his mother's flank. Catlicus the serpent-skirted caught a little ball of feathers from the sky and hid it in her bosom, and the Aztec god Huitzilopochtli was thus conceived. The virgin

---

[38] Matt. 27:52-53
[39] Luke 7:12-15
[40] John 11:43

Nana took a pomegranate from the tree watered by the blood of the slain Agdestris, and laid it in her bosom, and gave birth to the god Attis. The virgin daughter of a Mongol king awoke one night and found herself bathed in a great light, which caused her to give birth to Genghis Khan. Krishna was born of the virgin Devaka. Horus was born of the virgin Isis. Mercury was born of the virgin Maia. Romulus was born of the virgin Rhea Sylvia. For some reason, many religions forced themselves to think of the birth canal as a one-way street."[41]

- In Matthew 1:19-20, It seems that Joseph's first reaction is that of disbelief. He originally planned to hide her from the public. Why would he want to do that if he believed her story? To Joseph's credit, which is more believable, the creator of the universe planted his divine seed in a mortal, or a newly-married jewish teenager had a one night stand then told a lie that got *seriously* fucking out of control? Anyway, an angel allegedly intervenes and changes Joseph's mind.

- Great, but consider two things. First, why does the Bible trace Yeshua's lineage through the ancestry of *Joseph,* unless Joseph was *the actual birth father?* The lineage is actually traced twice in the Bible[42], with many glaring

---

[41] Christopher Hitchens, "God Is Not Great"

contradictions and fabrications between the two. Second, would it give you pause to know that the ideas of miraculous conception and virgin birth were not unique in the history of religion?

- Flavius Josephus is the earliest known source outside of the Bible. He wrote his account decades after Jesus' death. His one and only paragraph on Jesus[43] is commonly believed to be a forgery, inserted into a later edition by Eusebius in 325 C.E.[44] Josephus never met Jesus and never converted to Christianity, which raises suspicion that the following account attributed to him is authentic:

"Now there was about this time Jesus, a wise man, if it be lawful to call him a man; for he was a doer of wonderful works, a teacher of such men as receive the truth with pleasure. He drew over to him both

---

[42] Luke:23-38; Matt. 1:1-17

[43] His only other reference to Jesus was in passing: As therefore Ananus was of such a disposition, he thought he had now a good opportunity, as Festus was now dead, and Albinus was still on the road; so he assembled a council of judges, and brought before it the brother of Jesus the so-called Christ, whose name was James, together with some others, and having accused them as lawbreakers, he delivered them over to be stoned.

[44] "Eusebius confesses that he had included stories that would do credit to the glory of Christianity and he had suppressed all that could tend to discredit Christianity.", "Rise and Fall of the Roman Empire"

many of the Jews and many of the Gentiles. He was [the] Christ. And when Pilate, at the suggestion of the principal men amongst us, had condemned him to the cross, those that loved him at the first did not forsake him; for he appeared to them alive again the third day; as the divine prophets had foretold these and ten thousand other wonderful things concerning him. And the tribe of Christians, so named from him, are not extinct at this day."[45]

Bottom line, *no one* from Jesus' time wrote about him, his deeds, the resurrection, the earthquake, the zombies rising from the graveyard in Jerusalem, the eclipse, any of it. All the stories, including the Gospels and Paul's accounts, came 60 to 100 years later by people that never knew him personally.

- The Christian virgin birth is no more historical or believable than that of numerous other gods. Moreover, the idea of a Virgin-Mother-Goddess is practically universal. The list of Pagan virgin mothers include the following[46]:

1 Alcmene, mother of Hercules who gave birth on December 25th
2 Alitta, Babylonian Madonna and Child

---

[45] "Jewish Antiquities" 18.3.3

[46] http://www.truthbeknown.com/virgin.htm

46

3   Anat, Syrian wife of "the earlier Supreme God El," called "Virgin Goddess"
4   Cavillaca, Peruvian huaca (divine spirit) impregnated by the "son of the sun god" through eating his semen in the shape of a fruit
5   Chimalman, mother of Kukulcan
6   Chinese mother of Foe (Buddha)
7   Coatlicue, mother of the Mexican god Huitzilopochtli
8   Cybele, "Queen of Heaven and Mother of God"
9   Danae, mother of Perseus
10 Demeter/Ceres, "Holy Virgin" mother of Persephone/Kore and Dionysus
11 Devaki, mother of Krishna
12 Frigga, mother of the Scandinavian god Balder
13 Hera, mother of Zeus's children
14 Hertha, Teutonic goddess
15 Isis, who gave birth to Horus on December 25th
16 Juno, mother of Mars/Ares, called "Matrona" and "Virginalis," the Mother and Virgin
17 Mandana, mother of Cyrus/Koresh
18 Maya, mother of Buddha
19 Mother of Lao-kiun, "Chinese philosopher and teacher, born in 604 B.C."
20 Mother of the Indian solar god Rudra
21 Nana, mother of Attis
22 Neith, mother of Osiris, who was "worshipped as the Holy Virgin, the Great Mother, yet an Immaculate Virgin."
23 Nutria, mother of an Etruscan Son of God

24 Ostara, the German goddess

25 Rohini, mother of Indian "son of God"

26 Semele, mother of Dionysus/Bacchus, who was born on December 25th

27 Shin-Moo, Chinese Holy Mother

28 Siamese mother of Somonocodom (Buddha)

29 Sochiquetzal, mother of Quetzalcoatl

30 Vari, Polynesian "First Mother," who created her children "by plucking pieces out of her sides."

31 Venus, the "Virgo Coelestis" depicted as carrying a child

- Here is a homework assignment for you: Compare and contrast the *Slaughter of the Innocents* stories from the Old Testament (Moses) and the New Testament (Jesus). How do you account for the obvious similarities? Next, research the (extra biblical) historical evidence for both events. (Spoiler alert: You're going to find Jack shit)

We all fall short of the glory of God. We are all born into sin.

- Yahweh creates man and woman, <u>knowing</u> they would sin. Then he impregnates a Jewish teenager from Palestine with himself, so that he can be born as a man. Once alive, he kills himself to save you from the sin he <u>originally</u> <u>condemned</u> you to in the first place. Makes perfect sense.

Man condemned himself after disobeying the command of God.

- Put another way, the murder of an innocent man was required to save you from being found guilty, by an intelligent agent you've never met, of a crime that *someone else* committed. Apologists such as C. S. Lewis were proponents of the idea of the Law of Human Nature that we humans are intuitively aware of. If *scapegoating,* as mentioned above, seems counterintuitive, it therefore must be against the Law of Human Nature as well.

- It's one thing to buy into this delusion personally, but to teach a child, before she has reached the age of reason, that she is a dirty sinner is nothing less than brainwashing and cruel beyond measure. There is no such thing as a Catholic child, Muslim child or atheist child. Children are too young to know where they stand on this issue. Indoctrination at an early age is child abuse.

- A talking snake tricked a dirt-man and rib-woman into eating a piece of fruit. The fruit gave them the ability to know the difference between good and evil, right and wrong. Tell me, how were they supposed to know it was *wrong* to eat the fruit in the first place?

- Let me get this straight... Your god created everything that exists to celebrate *itself* and we should all happily devote our entire lives to sucking up to it because it has commanded us to do so. Further, if I don't kiss its ass with enough sincerity, frequency or enthusiasm, I have committed an unpardonable sin. Where do I sign up? Christians work in guilt as a master craftsman works in fine cabinetry!

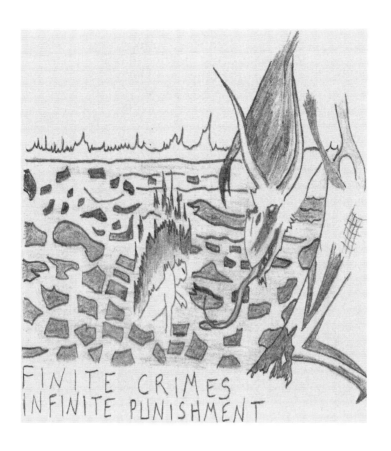

The universe and life on Earth are so complex, they must have been intelligently designed.

- This is a classic example of the *argument from ignorance* [47]fallacy of logic. To deny that a (scientifically proven) natural process is responsible for the existence of the complexity is to make a second logical fallacy, the *argument from incredulity*[48].

- "God did it" is not an explanation at all.

- Your god must be extraordinarily complex. Using the same line of logic, what created your god[49]?

  → States creation of eternal being

- Saying that God is eternal doesn't solve your dilemma. That is just unsubstantiated *special pleading*.

- Evolution through natural selection provides the best explanation for how complex organisms came into existence from simple organisms. The evidence for it is overwhelming. The fields of biology, geology, paleontology, genetics and chemistry all agree on this.

---

[47] "Look around at the trees, the mountains and all the complex organisms on Earth. Only God could have made all this. You can't definitively tell me he didn't. Therefore, God exists."
[48] "I cannot image how that could be possible. Therefore, it is not possible."
[49] See *Infinite Regress*

- Did your god just *decide* to design all the plants and animals in the complex hierarchy we observe, in which commonalities of both physical traits and DNA points unequivocally to their common ancestor? It would have had to do that just to fool us.

- Even if you could prove, beyond a shadow of a doubt, that an intelligent agent created the universe in its present form from nothing, all your heavy lifting still lies ahead of you. You must then sift through the thousands of gods that have ever been worshipped to prove it was *your* god that did it.

- Science has questions that may never be answered. Religion has answers that may never be questioned.

- Creationists love to bring up irreducible complexity. Therefore, it behooves you to know something about it and why it is deeply flawed pseudoscience. NOTE: Don't hold the creationist's hand and spoon-feed her tons of information. It will most likely end up becoming an exercise in futility anyway. What I have have provided here is more than enough to get her started toward learning the facts. Then, point her toward the mountains of research on the subject. A great place for her to start would be to read the court transcripts from the 2005

Kitzmiller v. Dover School District case. The scientists who testified as witnesses for the plaintiffs did a superb job in arguing against irreducible complexity in layman's terms. (Spoiler Alert) in Judge John Jones' 139-page decision, he hammered the creationists, using language such as "breathtaking inanity", "unconstitutional", "lie", "not a scientific theory", "outdated concepts", "cover their tracks" and "disguise the real purpose". Is Jones a liberal activist judge? He was appointed to the Federal Court by none other than George W. Bush! OK, (deep breath) here's the down-and-dirty version:

Irreducible complexity is the idea that animals, or parts of animals, are so complex that their existence cannot be explained by natural selection. In other words, the argument is that anything less that the complete form of an organ or organism would not be beneficial and therefore could not have come about by evolution. Some common examples cited by creationists are the eye, wing, bacterial flagellum, bombardier beetle, blood-clotting cascade and immune system. I will address the first three. Consider the remaining three your homework.

"What good is half of an eye?" The development of the eye most likely began with the evolution of light-receptive cells. A creature that can detect light has an obvious survival advantage over a completely blind creature. Over subsequent generations, the light-sensitive cells receded into into a depression, allowing the organism to better determine the direction of the light source. The depression became a pit, which allowed light to be focused onto individual photoreceptive cells, over time becoming a crude pinhole camera, allowing the organism to detect shapes. The hole in the camera eventually became a lens. From here, various branches of the evolutionary tree allowed some animals to see better at night, some to see long distances, some with forward-looking binocular vision for hunting, some with wide-angle vision for detecting approaching predators, and other with improved color vision or focusing mechanisms. The argument from incredulity loses all its traction when it is discovered that the eye has *independently evolved* numerous times over the history of the planet, perhaps between 50 and 100 separate times.[50] Not only was the natural development of the complex eye *possible,* it was statistically *inevitable.*

The wing. This example isn't used as frequently by creationists nowadays, probably due to the sheer number of recently-discovered

---

[50] Quiring, "Homology of the Eyeless Gene of Drosophila to the Small Eye in Mice and Aniridia in Humans" Science (1994); Haszprunar, "The Mollusca: Coelomate Turbellarians or Mesenchymate Annelids?" (1995)

transitional fossil specimens linking reptiles to birds.[51] As long as an environment remains stable, evolution grinds to a halt because all the species of plant and animal become fully adapted. When long-term changes in the environment occur however, that's when the real fun begins! Natural selection takes over to better adapt the current species to the new environment. One can imagine an increase in the population of land-based carnivores in an area and the obvious survival advantages of living in trees. Genetic mutations resulting in very minor changes in surface-volume ratio and air resistance allowed some animals to be able to effectively glide from tree to tree without having to expose themselves to the dangerous ground predators. Also, falling out of trees resulted in little to no injury. The early wings were not just good for gliding but were also used for insulation, to increase leaping ability and to attract mates. Any type of appendage even remotely resembling a wing would undoubtedly have had a wide range of useful applications.   - If you read the Kitzmiller v. Dover School District court transcripts or watch the Nova television program entitled "Judgment Day - Intelligent

---

[51] Notable examples include Protoavis, Archeopteryx, Hesperornis, Ichthyornis, Sinornis Santensis, Deinonychus, Oviraptor, Lisboasaurus Estesi, Coelophysis, and Ambiortus Dementjevi.

Design On Trial", both sides of the argument regarding the bacterial flagellum motor are laid out in detail. In a nutshell, creationists argue that because the bacteria in question has a propulsion unit (flagellum) which looks remarkably like a highly-complex rotating outboard motor, that any intermediate step leading up to it would be useless and therefore the flagellum would have never evolved. Well wouldn't you know, scientists have discovered flagellum precursors such as the Type III Secretory System[52], which were equally beneficial to the bacteria, only in other ways. Before it was a propulsion device, it was a needle used to infect healthy nearby organisms. Consider a mousetrap with a missing locking mechanism. You can't use it to catch mice, but it still works as a tie clasp!

---

[52] Salmond, Reeves, "Membrane Traffic Wardens and Protein Secretion in Gram-Negative Bacteria"; *Trends Biochem Sci* (1993)

"Turtles all the way down", used to illustrate the problem with the concept of infinite regress, is possibly rooted in ancient Hindu mythology, but is commonly attributed to Bertrand Russell and was made popular by Stephen Hawking in 1988. As the story usually goes, a professor is giving a lecture about Earth's orbit around the sun. A student stands up and exclaims "That is nonsense! The Earth rests on the back of a giant turtle (or an elephant followed by a turtle)". The professor retorts, "Well, if that's true, on what is the turtle standing?" The student answers, "It's turtles all the way down!"

Most people believe in God, can they *all* be wrong?

- This is a fallacy of logic commonly referred to as *appeal to the mob*.

- The fallacious *appeal to the mob* phrase "*vox populi vox Dei*", Latin for "*the voice of the people is the voice of God*"[53], appears in a famous quote by Charles Darwin:

"To suppose that the eye [...] could have been formed by natural selection seems, I freely confess, absurd in the highest degree. When it was first said that the sun stood still and the world turned round, the common sense of mankind declared the doctrine false; but the old saying of Vox populi, vox Dei, as every philosopher knows, cannot be trusted in science. Reason tells me, that if numerous gradations from a simple and imperfect eye to one complex and perfect can be shown to exist, each grade being useful to its possessor, as is certainly the case; if further, the eye ever varies and the variations be inherited, as is likewise certainly the case and if such variations should be useful to any animal under changing conditions of life, then the difficulty of believing that a perfect and complex eye could be formed by natural selection, though insuperable by our imagination, should not be considered as subversive of the theory."[54]

---

[53] http://www.merriam-webster.com/dictionary

[54] Charles Darwin, "On the Origin of Species by Means of Natural Selection, or the Preservation of Favoured Races in the Struggle for Life"

Christians love to quote-mine[55] this statement. By only reading the first sentence, apologists attempt to convince their audience that Darwin himself acknowledged the concept of *irreducible complexity* and had doubts regarding the regarding the veracity of his *own theory*.

- If you're talking about *your* god, the Hebrew war-god *Yahweh*, then no, most people on Earth *do not* believe in it.

- Most people *used* to believe that the Earth is the center of the solar system and the sun and planets revolved around it. Most people *used* to believe in astrology.

- Do *most Christians* believe in the Bible, a book that says the Earth is flat[56], disc-shaped, and the sky is made of metal with pin holes poked in it?[57]

- There are 1.6 billion Muslims on the planet[58], can *they* all be wrong? If so, *you are an atheist*

---

[55] The deceptive practice of quoting out of context, also referred to as "contextomy"

[56] Isa. 40:22

[57] "Firmament". The original word *raqia* is derived from the root *raqa*, meaning "to beat or spread out", e.g., the process of making a dish by hammering thin a lump of metal.

[58] "The Future of the Global Muslim Population", Pew Research Center (27 January 2011)

with regard to Islam. In fact, you are (presumably) atheistic towards all the thousands of religions that exist and have ever existed. It seems we have much more in common than you previously expected. The only difference is that I take it exactly one religion further than you! *As soon as you understand why you reject all other religions, you will understand why I reject yours.*

- A lie is a lie even if everyone believes it. The truth is the truth even if nobody believes it.

- "For me, it is far better to grasp the Universe as it really is than to persist in delusion, however satisfying and reassuring."[59]

- Homework assignment: Research the mass hysteria caused by the *Hindu Milk Miracle*. How is this occurrence relevant?

---

[59] Carl Sagan, "Cosmos" (1980)

I survived a horrific illness/disease/car wreck, and the only explanation is that it was a miracle. God was watching over me.

- Why does your god only heal some people but not others?

- Why wont your god heal amputees[60]? Why does it seem as though it is only concerned with *internal* diseases and illnesses? Show me one example of a remission, healing or recovery in which *the only possible explanation* is a supernatural intervention.

- With your ignorance of probability statistics, it's a "miracle" you haven't lost everything you own by now.

- If the odds of you winning the lottery are 14 million to 1, winning would quite possibly feel like a miracle. In a population of 300 million people however, the occurrence doesn't seem so miraculous. It is even less so when you take into account that an individual person can play the lottery hundreds, even thousands of times in their adult lifetime.

- You were involved in a vehicle collision? So are 6 million people every year. Only about 40,000 died as a result. That's six deaths out of every thousand people. Try again.

---

[60] A great source of information regarding this topic may be found at http://whywontgodhealamputees.com/.

- Imagine you are the sole survivor of a plane crash. About 200 people die, but you live. Your innate disposition toward *confirmation bias* might lead to you conclude that it was a miracle, that the almighty hand of God protected you from harm. Confirmation bias, or the tendency of humans to favor information that conforms to their strongly-held preconceived beliefs or notions, has a way of causing us to forget about or disregard any contrary information. In this case, everyone else that died. While your extremely relieved loved ones are on their knees thanking their deity for sparing you, they forget about the suffering families of the victims and no one holds their god accountable for the tragedy. Yahweh receives all the praise and none of the blame. It's either amazing grace, or "all part of God's plan".

- Let's pin down what we mean by a *miracle.* To paraphrase David Hume, a miracle is a supernatural interdiction which violates the laws of nature, or an interruption in the behavior of physical matter. The 10th chapter of Joshua tells us that Yahweh stopped the Sun for a period of about 24 hours so Joshua and his Israelites could finish slaughtering the Amorites in broad daylight. Yahweh also helped out by raining down meteors and impeding the Amorite retreat of innocent

women and children, which allegedly killed more of the enemy than did the Israelites. Now, for the sake of argument, I will pretend that the author of Joshua was not a geocentrist and what he meant
was that Yahweh stopped the *rotation of the Earth*. In doing that, many additional miracles would have to occur, not least of which would be preventing every person on the planet from slamming into fixed objects at about half the speed of sound, given the fact that the Earth is spinning at roughly 1,000 mph at the equator. This chain of necessary lesser miracles continues, but I will stop because my head is already spinning from the ridiculousness of this story.

- Mark 11:24 says "Therefore I tell you, whatever you ask for in prayer, believe that you have received it, and it will be yours." This promise appears throughout the Bible.[61] Sounds easy enough, so why do miracles so seldom come to pass? Of all the apologetic excuses I have heard to explain away this obvious dilemma, not one has been even remotely satisfactory.

- In biblical times, there were pillars of smoke, turning a staff into a snake, an impossible flood, living inside the belly of a whale[62] for

---

[61] Matt. 7:7, 17:20, 21:21; John 3:16, 14:14

three days, people raised from the dead, turning water into wine, parting seas, people fed manna from Heaven, a virgin birth, plagues and pestilence, and walking on water. Nowadays, all it takes to constitute a miracle is a cancer remission or surviving a vehicle rollover? Did the status of *miracles* get severely downgraded in the last 2000 years? Yes, a lost child found in the woods after three days or a crew of miners being rescued from a collapsed tunnel can be highly improbable occurrences, but a *miracle*?

- Carl Sagan called this mistake the *Texas sharpshooter fallacy*. The marksman takes shot at the side of a barn and then draws a target around the bullet hole in the wall. "Look, another bulls eye!!! Damn I'm a good shot!"

---

[62] Yes, I know it was a "big fish" and not a whale. Does that make the story the least bit more believable?

You don't *want* to believe in God! You just deny God so you have an excuse to commit sins.

- What about atheists that grew up in India? Do they *not want* to believe in Shiva?

- Lack of belief is not a cop-out, this is what is known as the Null Hypothesis.□ It is the default position to take on claims for which there is insufficient demonstrable evidence and reasoned argument to support the claim.

- In the United States, atheists constitute 0.2% of the prison population[63] and 67% of all scientists[64]. Belief in God is as low as 5.5% among biologists and 7.5% among physicists and astronomers. And we *all* know how violent, sadistic and immoral those science-geeks are, right?

- *Sin*, by definition, is a crime against a god. Atheists don't accept a god hypothesis because there is insufficient evidence for it. *Without a god* is inherently *without sin*. It's also a life without the guilt of Original Sin, a life free from atonement for the iniquities of our ancestors, and a life free from the threat of eternal damnation.

---

[63] Federal Bureau of Prisons, 5 March 1997

[64] Pew Research Center for the People & the Press, May and June 2009

Imagine No Religion

God answers my prayers.

- Then why are there so many starving children on the planet?

- How can a loving god ignore the prayers of the innocent and faithful?

- Why do bad things happen to good people who pray? Catastrophic events befall people of faith every day. Either your god can do nothing to stop catastrophes, it doesn't care to, or it doesn't exist. Your god is either impotent, evil, or imaginary. Take your pick, and choose wisely. The only way sense to make of these tragedies is that bad things happen to innocent people. This understanding inspires compassion. Religious faith, on the other hand, erodes compassion. Justifications like "this is all part of God's plan", "there are no accidents in life", or "people always get what they deserve in the end" - these ideas are not only stupid, they are extraordinarily callous. They are a childish refusal to connect with the suffering of other human beings. It is time to grow up and let our hearts break for the victims of tragedy.

- In the case of marriages, "what God has put together, let no man put asunder". So why do Christians get divorced at the same rate as everybody else? Praying for a successful marriage, and your god sanctifying it, makes no difference whatsoever.

- If prayers were really answered, we would expect that people who pray should have significantly better lives than those who don't pray. A lifetime of prayer should lead to increased fortune, happiness, faster rates of healing, reduced occurrences of disease amongst themselves and their loved ones, or any other clear indication that spiritual assistance has been attained. No matter who you pray to, or how often you pray, all scientific tests lead to the same conclusion: It is as effective as random chance. In other words, prayer has no effect whatsoever.[65]

---

[65] "Statistical Inquiries Into The Efficacy Of Prayer", Fortnightly Review, vol. 12, 1872; "The Objective Efficacy Of Prayer", Journal of Chronic Diseases vol. 18, 1965; "An Experimental Study of the Effects of Distant, Intercessory Prayer on Self-Esteem, Anxiety, and Depression", "Intercessory Prayer in the Treatment of Alcohol Abuse and Dependence: A Pilot Investigation", Alternative Therapies in Health and Medicine; "Intercessory Prayer and Cardiovascular Disease Progression in a Coronary Care Unit Population: A Randomized Controlled Trial", Mayo Clinic Proceedings, 2001; "Study of the Therapeutic Effects of Intercessory Prayer in Cardiac Bypass Patients", American Heart Journal, 2006

God speaks to me personally.

- Are you impressed when a person tells you they were abducted by aliens or saw a ghost? *That's* how I find *your* claims.

- When one person sees or hears something that isn't there, it's called a delusion. When a small group of people have the same experience, it's a cult. Millions of people? Religion.

- You simply hear what you want to hear. Believers in other religions think *their* god talks to *them* as well.

- Andrea Yates, a suburban mother in Houston Texas, drowned her five children, one by one, in her bathtub. She indicated that she had spoken with God and believed he would "take them up." When she was asked what might have happened if she had not taken their lives. "I guess they would have continued stumbling. They would have gone to hell." She was sentenced to life in prison. Compare this to the stories of Abraham and Isaac in Genesis 22:5, or Jephthah and his daughter in Judges 11:39.

- In Canada, July 2008, Vince Weiguang Li said he had heard what he believed was "the voice of God" instructing him as he beheaded a fellow

Greyhound bus passenger. Li went on to indicated that he was the second coming of Jesus.

- What are we to make of these types of stories? Sigmund Freud had perhaps the most logical take on the issue: "There is no other source of knowledge of the universe, but the intellectual manipulation of carefully verified observations, in fact, what is called research, and that no knowledge can be obtained from revelation, intuition or inspiration." Freud regarded religion as simply an illusion and wishful thinking not grounded on scientific research or knowledge. To Freud, religion is a system of wishful illusions and a denial of reality, a state of blissful hallucinatory confusion.

- "I swear guys, I've got an invisible friend who watches me from the sky, and when I think of him really hard, he grants me wishes!" "Shut up and take your meds."

That was the *Old* Testament. Those laws don't apply to us anymore.

- The *Ten Commandments* are in the Old Testament, are *they* obsolete as well? Incidentally, the ten *laws* that rednecks are always fighting to bring into public schools and courthouses aren't the *actual Ten Commandments*. Moses went up Mount Sinai several times. Not until the last time did he come back with these "Ten Commandments", written on the stones[66]:

1   Obey the commandments. Yahweh will conquer the Amorites, Canaanites, Hittites, Perizzites, Hivites, and Jebusites. Be careful not to make a treaty with those who live in the land where you are going, or they will be a snare among you. Break down their altars, smash their sacred stones, and cut down their Asherah poles.

2   Do not worship any other god, for Yahweh, whose name is Jealous, is a jealous god. Do not make treaties with those in other lands who worship other gods.

3   Do not make cast idols.

---

[66] Don't believe me? Read Exodus 20 through 34:28 and count how many times Moses goes up the mountain, when the tablets are actually *created*, destroyed and created again exactly as before. Note when the phrase "The Ten Commandments" appears in the story. You will see which ten of the 613 laws are the *actual* Commandments. Yes, Deuteronomy 5 lists the standard Ten Commandments, but the author never refers to them as such.

4   Celebrate the Feast of Unleavened Bread. For seven days eat bread made without yeast during the first month of the Hebrew Year.

5   Sacrifice the firstborn of every womb, including all the firstborn males of your livestock. You can sacrifice a lamb in place of a firstborn donkey but if you do sacrifice the donkey break its neck. If your firstborn child is a boy sacrifice something else in its place. None shall appear before Yahweh without a sacrifice.

6   Do not work on the sabbath, even during the plowing season and harvest you must rest.

7   Celebrate the Jewish holiday "The Feast of Weeks" with the firstfruits of the wheat harvest and celebrate the Jewish holiday "The Feast of Ingathering" at the turn of the year. Three times a year all your men are to appear before the god of Israel and he will conquer surrounding nations before you enlarging your territory.

8   Do not mix blood sacrifices to Yahweh with yeast and do not let any sacrifice from the Passover Feast remain until morning.

9   Bring the firstfruits of your land to the house of Yahweh, your god.

10 Do not cook a baby goat in his mother's milk.

- The phrase "Ten Commandments", incidentally, is only uttered twice in Bible and they both relate to *these ten laws only*. The ten laws that most people are used to seeing are part of the 613 Jewish laws, and those were *only spoken* to Moses. *He did not write them down.*

- The Bible clearly states that the laws, commandments and prohibitions in the Old Testament will *always* apply and will *never* become outdated[67].

- Jesus himself admitted the old laws still apply[68] , until the Earth is destroyed.

- Why is the Old Testament even still part of the Bible then? Why did the early Christian church followers include it in the canon?

- Without the Old Testament, there is no reason whatsoever for Jesus' vicarious redemption. If the Old Testament doesn't apply, there is no original sin, no unnecessary dietary laws, no Ten Commandments to follow and the rest of the 613 old laws don't apply. You can't cherry-pick the parts of the old law you think are still relevant and trash the rest. By doing that, you are admitting that humans have an innate sense of morality and the Bible is not necessary at all. I'll say it again because it

---

[67] Deut. 4:2; Gen. 17:19; Exod. 12:14, 17, 24; Lev. 23:14,21,31; Deut. 4:8-9; Deut. 7:9; Deut. 11:1, 26-28;
[67]1 Chron. 16:15; Psalm 119:151-2, 160; Ecc. 12:13; Malachi 4:4; Matt. 5:18-19; Luke 16:17
[68] Matt. 5:17-18, Luke 16:17; John 7:19, John 10:35

bears repeating: According to the dozen Bible verses I previously cited, *the Old Testament will always apply and will never become outdated*. Additionally, even most believers agree that the Old Testament was not meant to be a historical record, but instead it is simply for Christians and Jews to gain insight into ancient culture, mythology and morality. So here we are, with the historicity and morality subtracted, we are left with a book on ancient culture and mythology. We may now place in on the shelf next to Homer, Sophocles and Strabo, devoid of divine inspiration.

- The Yahweh of the Old Testament is the same Yahweh of the New Testament. Did this new and improved Yahweh 2.0 change his all-knowing mind and decide to change what is morally good and bad? If a believer argues that morality is indeed objective and stays the same throughout time, he is now met with a serious dilemma. One common reply to this critique is the concept of *dispensations*.

- Saying "oh, but that was a different time and a different place" just proves my point that there is no such thing as objective morality. Thanks, but get back over on your side of the argument, I don't need any help.

The Old Testament Doesn't Apply.

Unless of course we say it
applies then the part we say
applies does apply but the
bad stuff you mentioned
doesn't apply because of
Jesus.

The Bible is the perfect, infallible word of God.

- Yahweh did *not* create the universe in six days, 6,000 years ago.

- There was *never* a worldwide flood that covered Mt. Everest.

- Yahweh did *not* create Adam from a handful of dust and Eve from a rib.

- Jonah did *not* live inside a fish's stomach for three days.

- No human has *ever* lived for 150 years, much less 969[69] years.

- The Book of Didache was once part of the New Testament, but later removed. The concept of the trinity wasn't established until almost 200 years after the death of Jesus and the New Testament itself wasn't even put together until around 350 C.E. How many copying errors do you think were made during that time? Did the Council of Nicea in 325 correctly decide on Jesus' divinity and his relationship to Yahweh? Should any of the dozens of Nag Hammadi codices have been included? Did the Council of Trent make a grave mistake when they canonized the 14 apocryphal books in 1546? *Perfect* and *infallible* are definitely not two two

---

[69] Methuselah, Gen 5:27

of the adjectives I would use when describing the Bible.

- The Bible was allegedly written by men who were anointed with the spirit of Yahweh itself to reveal a sacred message. This amounts to nothing more that hearsay, which does not hold up as evidence. L. Ron Hubbard, Joseph Smith, Muhammad and hundreds more have made the exact same claim. Is the divinely-inspired authorship of Scientology, Mormonism or Islam any less believable? If so, why? Do you not see this as a double standard?

- Ok, we come now to the myriad contradictions in the Bible. *Complete* listings of biblical contradictions have already been published elsewhere[70], so I will just point out a few of my favorites:
1 God doesn't get angry[71], God's anger lasts for just a moment[72], God's anger lasts a long time[73] , God's anger doesn't last forever[74], God's anger lasts forever[75].

---

[70] "The Bible Handbook" by G. W. Foote and W. P. Ball; "Skeptics Annotated Bible",
http://skepticsannotatedbible.com/contra/by_name.html;
http://www.1001biblecontradictions.com/
[71] Judith 8:15
[72] Psalm 30:5
[73] Num. 32:13
[74] Jer. 3:12, Micah 7:18
[75] Jer. 17:4, Malachi 1:4, Matt. 25:41, Matt. 25:46

2   On what did Jesus ride into Jerusalem? On a colt[76]? On a young ass[77]? Or both at the same time[78]?

3   When did Jesus ascend into heaven? On the day of his resurrection[79]? At least eight days after his resurrection[80]? Or forty days after his resurrection[81]?

4   Divorce is never permissible[82]. Only permissible when the wife is unfaithful[83]. Only when the 'unbelieving' partner chooses to leave[84]. Only when the husband is displeased with his wife[85].

5   Is God the creator of evil? Yes[86], or no[87]?

• Matthew 1:6-16: Here we learn that there are 28 generations in a bloodline from King David to Jesus. Two problems: First, Luke 3:23-31 has the two separated by 43 generations. Only three names in the two lists are the same. Second, why is it so important to show that

---

[76] Mark 11:7

[77] John 12:14

[78] Matt. 21:5-7

[79] Luke 24:1-51, Mark 16:9-19

[80] John 20:26

[81] Acts 1:2-3, 9

[82] Matt. 19:6, Mark 10:11, Luke 16:18

[83] Matt. 5:32, Matt. 19:9

[84] 1 Cor. 7:15

[85] Deut. 24:1-2

[86] 2 Kings 6:33, Isa. 45:7, Lam. 3:38, Amos 3:6

[87] Psalm 5:4, 1 John 4:8

Yeshua is a descendant of David unless, of course, *Joseph* was actually his biological father? If *Yahweh* is the father, why list this genealogy? Hmm, if Jesus got his Y chromosome from God, I would love to study a hair sample! What does immortal DNA look like I wonder!

You just need to have an open mind.

- Having good critical thinking skills does not mean I am close-minded.

- Be wary, the same mental process that sucks people into believing in gods also goes for ghosts, alien abductions, crop circles, bigfoot, Loch Ness monster and so on.

- A window stuck open is even more useless that a window stuck closed.

- Atheists have the education and intellect to accept facts and live in reality. They deny the existence of gods in the absence of material proof but they can still discuss the matter. Aristotle said "It is the mark of an educated mind to be able to entertain a thought without accepting it." But why are Christians unable (or unwilling) to contemplate the non-existence of a god? Lack of education? Intellect? Could it just be the child abuse of having religion forced into them at a very, very early age and the lack the ability to escape that indoctrination?! Religion is like a penis – It's ok to have one, it's ok to be proud of it. But it's *not* ok to wave it around in public or try to shove it down children's throats!

- I could be wrong about your religion. We could *both* be wrong about every other religion that has ever existed. For all I know, we could both be wrong about the Supreme Brahma (a superior creation myth in my opinion) for example. Which is more likely, that the natural order of the universe sometimes gets thrown out the window to answer your prayers, or you are under a grave misapprehension?

The New Testament is trustworthy in terms of the history it tells us. The Gospels are rooted in eyewitness testimony.

- No New Testament original documents exist.

- What we do have are translated Greek copies, made centuries[88] after Yeshua[89] died.

- All of the 5,700 fragments and full-length Greek copies are different from one another.

- The gospels were written anonymously. The names Matthew, Mark, Luke and John were attached to the stories much later.

- The first gospel, Mark, was written about 50 years after Yeshua's death. The oldest copy in existence today is dated at approximately 200 C.E. Imagine how skewed the original book of Mark must have become over 150 years of oral transmission!

- The gospel writers were not eyewitnesses. Yeshua had died decades earlier. The common agreement is that the authors were upper-class Greek scholars. Yeshua's disciples were illiterate.

- For such a supposedly important revelation, why didn't Yeshua ensure that future

---

[88] Bart Ehrman, "How The Bible Got Changed" speech, Stanford University 2011
[89] AKA Jesus

generations would receive his actual, unaltered words?

- In 1707, John Mill at Oxford spent 30 years looking at 100 different versions of the New Testament, trying to decide which version to print. When he had finished, he had noted over 30,000 places where the manuscripts differed from one another[90].

- What's so special about the teachings of Yeshua anyway? Nearly all of his tenants are so obvious that many other cultures had them centuries before Yeshua was even born. Virtually every moral "revelation" ever attributed to him was directly borrowed from older religions and texts.

---

[90] Mill didn't cite all the differences he found, only the ones he felt were significant!

Why do you use the Lord's name in vain when you don't even believe in him?

- I say words like *Easter Bunny*, *Mithra*, *Mother Goose* and the *Flying Spaghetti Monster* too; it doesn't mean I *believe* in them!

- Though I do not believe in your deity, I will still say something along the lines of "god dammit" or "Jesus Christ" because they are phrases embedded in social culture. They are more for the effect, or to add emphasis to a statement, and don't hold any religious connotations for me.

- Mainly due to reflex. Growing up in a religious world means that you learn to use those so-called *curses* when you are young, making it hard to "unlearn" them when you are older.

- I guess, when I stub my toe, I could try to get used to saying "by the beard of Zeus!" instead, but why replace one fictional character with another?

- Exactly what does it mean to "take the name of the Lord thy God in vain" anyway? Even Christians can't agree. Some have argued its using the name of their god in a frivolous way. Others say it only means using of the name of their god in occult or pagan rituals. The most common interpretation amongst theology scholars, however, is breaking a contract that was sworn in the name of their god.[91] Not exactly what the sheep are being taught on Sunday mornings, is it?

- Quick tangent: Unless I'm invoking the name of [insert fictional deity here], you can't argue that I am *swearing* or *cursing*. Therefore, there must be some other secular reason why a word like *shit* offends people. If someone know why that is, please enlighten me.

- Replacement words aren't any better. When someone says "the 'N' word", what's the first thing that pops into your head? Nigger. No matter how hard you try to get around actually saying nigger, the person you are talking to will always think *nigger*. If you want your friend to look at the full moon, you might use your hand to point to it. Once your friend sees the moon, your hand is no longer needed. The goal is the same no matter what you use to point at the moon. It could be a tree branch, a shoe or a tent pole, the outcome will be the same: Your friend will look at the moon. Keep this in mind whenever you hear a Christian saying "G-D", "gosh", "B-S", "darn it" or "shoot". They are embedding the *actual* so-called swear words in other peoples' heads and they don't even

---

[91]The Exodus version is translated as "in a vain oath", and the Deuteronomy version is translated as "in a false oath."

91

realize it. "Shut the front door"? Do us a favor and shut the fuck up.

- Words are just words. They convey meaning. Some years ago, I was somehow talked into going to a country and western nightclub with some friends. I hate country music, but I was trying to impress a girl (I even bought some Wranglers and took two weeks worth of two-step and waltz lessons at the local YMCA). That night was the first (and only) time I've climbed onto a mechanical bull. It ended badly. As I limped over to my friends afterwards, I commented that when I was being bucked forward off the bull, my asshole viciously grazed the saddlehorn. You know what puts a damper on the evening worse than a bruised asshole? A stranger yelling at you in public that she is offended by your obscene language. I look back on that encounter and wonder, would she have said anything if I had said "butthole" instead? How about just "ass"? I guess "whale eye" or "chocolate starfish" would have *really* set her off! My point is, they all mean the same thing. They are just words. *Asshole* is a word. *Fuck, cunt* and *meekrob*[92] are just words. Don't be afraid of them. It's all about the *intent* of the word, not the word itself. If you don't know the

---

[92] A Thai dish consisting of shrimp, noodles and pork belly. Also, the dirtiest word in the history of mankind, according to the animated t.v. series "South Park".

difference between saying you have a bruised asshole (I'm still laughing right now) and *calling someone* an asshole, there's no hope for you anyway. Oh, that girl I was trying to impress? We're now coming up on our 17th wedding anniversary!

If you don't believe in God, you have no moral compass to guide you. What is stopping you from committing crimes?

- Long before the time of Moses there were *governments*. Governments are founded upon *law*. Law is founded upon *moral codes*.

- In the Bible, Yahweh advocates genocide[93], incest[94], murder[95], slavery[96] and infanticide.[97] Is this *really* what you have chosen as the source of *your* morality?

- If your god commanded you to kill your child, would you do it? [98] Do you follow the laws prescribed by your god because you know them to be moral or out of fear of an ultimate authority, regardless of whether you think the laws are moral?

- Humans are mammals, not great white sharks. We have evolved to live within societies. All human societies have similar basic norms of moral conduct. According to Marc Hauser, professor of evolutionary biology at Harvard University, basic morality is genetically cultivated, naturally highly resistant to religious influence, and most people easily *reject*

---

[93] 1 Sam. 15; Deut 20:10-18

[94] There were on eight humans on the ark. I'll let you draw your own conclusions.

[95] Lev. 20:13; 2 Chron. 15:12-13; Jer. 48:10

[96] Col. 3:22; Lev. 25:44

[97] Num. 31:17; Hos. 13:16; 1 Sam. 15:3; Psalms 135:8, 136:10, 137:9

[98] Gen. 22:5 and 22:8; Judges 11:3-39

religious rules that violate their basic moral intuitions.[99]

- Morality *predates* the Bible[100]:
1   "Do not do to your neighbor what you would take ill from him." - Pittacus
2   "Avoid doing what you would blame others for doing." - Thales
3   "What you do not want to happen to you, do not do it yourself either." - Sextus the Pythagorean
4   "Do not do to others what would anger you if done to you by others." - Isocrates
5   "What thou avoidest suffering thyself seek not to impose on others." - Epictetus
6   "It is impossible to live a pleasant life without living wisely and well and justly (agreeing 'neither to harm nor be harmed), and it is impossible to live wisely and well and justly without living a pleasant life." - Epicurus
7   "One should never do wrong in return, nor mistreat any man, no matter how one has been mistreated by him." - Plato's Socrates (Crito, 49c)
8   "One who, while himself seeking happiness, oppresses with violence other beings who also

---

[99] "The Origins Of Religion : Evolved Adaptation Or By-Product?", Trends In Cognitive Sciences, Volume 14, Issue 3, March 2010, Pgs. 104–109
[100] All these predate Luke 6:31: "Do to others as you want them to do to you".

desire happiness, will not attain happiness hereafter." - Dhammapada 10. Violence

- I cannot speak for all atheists, but as for me and *every atheist I know*, we get our morality from a rational consideration of the consequences of our actions. I am conscious of the fact that my actions have an effect on those around me, and theirs have an effect on me. To live cooperatively with the rest of society, I have chosen to be perform actions that have a positive impact on others, while avoiding actions that could have a negative impact on them.

- Atheists tend to acquire their moral standards from an *acknowledgment of reality*, not from the *assertion of authority*.

- If, hypothetically, we knew for a fact that no gods existed, would you be tempted to run out and commit crimes? Is that your true nature? Only religion could allow otherwise normal, rational, moral people to entertain such *depraved* thoughts, let alone convince people that such thoughts are anywhere close to moral and ethical.

- Do you follow laws only out of fear of punishment and not because you know it's the right thing to do?

- All cultures of the world, throughout history, have had codes of conduct and many of these codes predate the writing of the Bible. Where did the Greek Philosophers gain their insights? Did Socrates have no morals? Was Pythagoras lost? Confucius? Buddha? Inuits? Native Americans?

- Is the Bible is a good source for morals?:
1 Kill gays, adulterers, disobedient children, non-Christians.
2 Wisdom teeth, tail bones, goose bumps, male nipples, eyebrows, appendix, toenails, eyes that see the world upside-down, esophagus too close to trachea. Intelligent design.
3 Help actress win awards. Do nothing about world hunger.
4 I am all powerful. Take day off to rest.
5 Allow humans to exist in completely isolated jungle-tribes. Send them to hell for not being Christian.
6 Create gravity. Forget to mention it.
7 Everything happens for a reason. Not tellin'.
8 Create Satan. Blame Satan.
9 Create universe. Wait 13.7 billion years to tell some isolated people in the desert what to do.
10 Telescopes getting more powerful. Time to move further away from Earth.
11 Create imperfect world. To showcase own perfection.

12 Demand Adam and Eve follow a rule that requires the understanding of right and wrong. Don't give them the knowledge of right and wrong.

13 Jews are my chosen people. Holocaust.

14 Accidentally makes humans too smart. They stop believing in me.

15 Love thy neighbor. Command them to slaughter each other.

- The Bible is perhaps the poorest source of morality imaginable. The atrocities that Yahweh permits, commits and demands of its followers are almost too numerous to count[101].

- Did the Israelites think it was morally acceptable to murder, steal and lie prior to Moses running down a mountain with a couple of stone tablets? *What*, I ask you, stopped those two million people from committing crimes prior to receiving divine instruction?

- Do you kill disobedient children, homosexuals, people who work on the Sabbath or eat shellfish? If a voice in your head told you to stab your son and then set him on fire, would you do it? Do you think slavery is morally justifiable[102]?

---

[101] Exod. 35:2, Lev. 20:13, Deut. 21:18-21, Deut. 22:13-21, and hundreds more

[102] Exod. 21:20, Eph. 6:5, 1 Peter 2:18, according to Jesus Col.

- According to the Bible, if you become the victim of a rape, your attacker must simply pay your father a small fine. Oh, and you have to marry the rapist[103].

- For the sake of argument, assume Christianity and the Bible never existed. What kind of person would you be? Would you commit wanton crimes, steal from others, or kill indiscriminately? If the only thing that keeps you from going on a murderous rampage is your belief in a god, then you need to seek psychiatric therapy immediately.

- Homo Sapiens have evolved a sense of empathy which inherently rejects the ideas of torture, slavery, genocide and cruelty to others.

- The book of Exodus tells the story of Moses, who led 600,000 men (as many as 2 million people including women and children) out of Egyptian bondage, wandered the desert for 40 years, arrived at Mount Sinai and delivered a sacred law to his followers, in the form   of ten commandments etched into stone by the hand of God. Strictly speaking, there has never been any clear evidence discovered in Egypt, or elsewhere, to support the Israelite Exodus from

---

3:22
[103] Deut. 22:28-29

Egypt, though there is no small amount of conjecture and theories. In fact today, Egyptologists, archaeologists and even Jewish scholars doubt the whole biblical story[104]. One expert is quoted as saying about the dilemma "If they get upset, I don't care. This is my career as an archaeologist. I should tell them the truth. If the people are upset, that is not my problem"[105].

- But, for the sake of argument, let's assume the story is historically accurate. God's children lived, grew old, and died for thousands years. They learned to live together in societies and presumably invented tribal rules on their own to maintain order. Then, around 1209 BCE, God intervenes and bestows the Ten Commandments and over 600 additional laws.

- From where did the australopithecus afarensis[106] get *their* morality?

- Why do modern day Christians consistently cherry-pick the Bible? Slavery was acceptable (even in the New Testament), why is it no

---

[104] Finegan, "Archaeological History of the Ancient Middle East"

[105] Slackman, New York Times, Published 3 April 2007

[106] The australopiths played an important part in human evolution. The australopith species eventually evolved into the Homo genus, of which humans belong, in Africa around two million years ago.

longer? Killing a woman if, on her wedding night, she is found to not be a virgin was absolutely OK. The brutal murder of disobedient teenagers; homosexuals, practitioners of the Wiccan faith, non-believers, people that gather firewood on the Sabbath, and children for making fun of a man's bald head… all were once completely sanctioned! Is your "unalterable, inerrant word of God" subject to revision or is it not?

- *Morality is subjective*, and evolves based on time period and geographical location. How much longer will you continue to insist that your morality comes from an archaic iron age text?

- We, like the other primates (and most other mammals for that matter), are social animals and have developed societies in which each member knows its own place. Social order is maintained by certain rules of expected behavior and dominant group members enforce order through punishment.

- Where do I get my morality? What's stopping me from committing crimes? My *hard-wired, genetic instincts*, combined with the fact that I am a Homo Sapien with a developed neocortex and am *capable of establishing a personal ethical code and living by it*. What you call "The Golden Rule" is a great example.

Christians didn't invent that concept. Far from it. The idea treating others as you would be treated predates Christianity and appears in dozens of older religions. It is a product of our evolutionary tribal heritage.

- Religious people can act morally, not *because* of their faith, but in *spite* of it.

- So, while you're breaking donkey's necks[107] and killing your kids, I'll be over here in the 21st Century helping to further human knowledge, battle disease, end poverty, and fight against injustice.

- Kill gays, adulterers, disobedient children, non-Christians. Wisdom teeth, tail bones, goose bumps, male nipples, eyebrows, appendix, toenails, eyes that see the world upside-down, esophagus too close to trachea = Intelligent design.

- Help actress win awards. Do nothing about world hunger.

---

[107] See the chapter "That was the *Old* Testament. Those laws don't apply to us anymore."

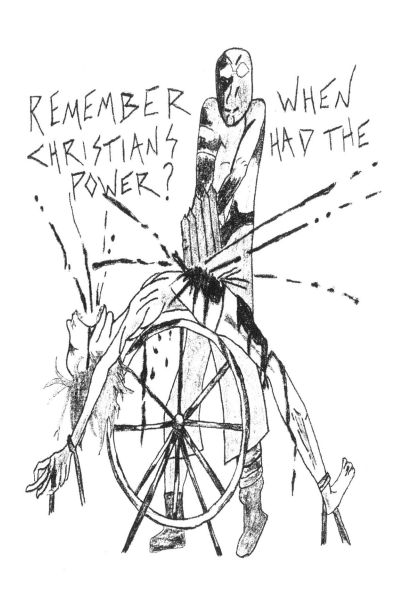

Did you *see* the big bang with your own eyes? Then you can't know for sure that God didn't create the universe.

- Did *you* see a god creating the universe? Have *you* ever seen a person spontaneously pop into existence? Then, using your own line of bad logic, *you* can't know *either*.

- The orbital period of Pluto is 248 Earth years.[108] We have known this fact for much less than 248 years. We have not yet observed Pluto make one full rotation around the sun, but we *know* it will take 248 years. There are many, *many* more tools in a scientist's toolbox than visual observation.

- Our universe is composed of roughly 25% dark matter and roughly 70% dark energy.[109] Everything we can see, planets, stars, galaxies, a tree in Central Park, is all but completely irrelevant and insignificant. 99.9999999999999% of the entire known universe is uninhabitable by humans. Does *this* sound like your intelligent creator had *us* in mind?

---

[108] NASA Goddard Space Flight Center
[109] "Seven-Year Wilson Microwave Anisotropy Probe (WMAP) Observations: Sky Maps, Systematic Errors, and Basic Results" nasa.gov.http://lambda.gsfc.nasa.gov/product/map/dr4/pub_pap ers/sevenyear/basic_results/wmap_7yr_basic_results.pdf. Retrieved 2010-12-02.

The universe is finely tuned for life. Strong evidence for a designer comes from the fine-tuning of the universal constants and the solar system.

- "The universe is not fine-tuned to life. Life is fine-tuned to the universe."[110]

- The "multiverse" theory is gaining ground. Most cosmologists are on board with this idea now. "...Completely different kinds of universes, with

[110] Victor J. Stenger, "The Fallacy Of Fine-Tuning"

different physics, different histories, maybe different numbers of spatial dimensions. Most will be sterile, although some will be teeming with life. A chief proponent of this... multiverse is Alexander Vilenkin, who paints a dramatic picture of an infinite set of universes with an infinite number of galaxies, an infinite number of planets and an infinite number of people with your name who are reading this article."[111] This can be explained if ours is just one universe in a "multiverse" - an infinite number of universes, each with different physical parameters. We would then have ended up in the one where the laws of physics are fine-tuned to life.

- Weak Anthropic Principle: If the universe was not the way it is, we would not be the way we are. In other words, if the forces of nature prevented any type of life from existing, there would be no sentient creatures around to *claim* that the universe is fine-tuned!

- Strong Anthropic Principle: The Universe must have those properties which allow life to develop within it at some stage in its history

- Suppose you were sentenced to death. You're tied to a stake, blindfolded, and you're told that there are 100 expert riflemen that will be

[111] Scientific American, "Does The Multiverse Really Exist?", 19 July 2011

shooting at you. They've never missed. "Ready, aim, *fire!*" You hear the shots, but you're not dead. How would you explain it? Did they all conspire to miss you? Did all the rifles jam? Did they all accidentally miss you? When you take off the blindfold, you realize that there were 101 prisoners!

- The claim that the physical constants that exist in the universe are so finely-tuned to allow the possibility of life to exist, that only an intelligent agency could have created the universe is a fallacy of logic known as *selection bias*. However, only in a universe capable of eventually supporting life will there even *be* living beings in existence to observe the "fine tuning", while a universe less compatible with life will go unwitnessed.

- Here is a great example of selection bias at work: Imagine a puddle waking up one morning and thinking, "This is an interesting world I find myself in — an interesting hole I find myself in — fits me rather neatly, doesn't it? In fact it fits me staggeringly well, must have been made to have me in it!" This is such a powerful idea that as the sun rises in the sky and the air heats up and as, gradually, the puddle gets smaller and smaller, it's still frantically hanging on to the notion that everything's going to be alright, because this world was meant to have him in it, was built to have him in it; so the moment he disappears catches him rather by surprise. I think this may be something we need to be on the watch out for. We all know that at some point in the future the Universe will come to an end and at some other point, considerably in advance from that but still not immediately pressing, the sun will explode. We feel there's plenty of time to worry about that, but on the other hand that's a very dangerous thing to say.[112]

---

[112] Douglas Adams, speech at Digital Biota 2, Cambridge, UK 1998

*E*volution is only a *theory.*

- Yes, just like the Theory of Gravity, the Germ Theory of Disease and Atomic Theory.

- The word *theory* has two meanings. In the casual everyday sense, a theory can mean a well thought out hypothesis ("I have a theory about what happened to my car keys.") in the scientific sense, however, a theory denotes a group of propositions and explanations supported by a *body of facts*. The theory of evolution is supported by a mountain of facts, such as:

1 Life has existed on earth for more than two billion years.
2 Species change and diversify over time.
3 All species have evolved from a common ancestor.
4 The engine that drives evolution is known as *natural selection*.

- A scientific theory is one formed around and therefore supported by the current evidence. The more evidence gathered, the stronger the theory. Evolution by means of natural selection, for example, is one of the strongest theories around as it currently dominates as the only one with actual evidence. This is a non-random process which causes genetic traits to become either more or less common within a species, or between species, over time and successive generations.

- Evolution is confirmed by every field of natural science. To call it the foundation of biology is an understatement. Here are some examples:
1 Evolution reproduced in the lab or documented in nature
2 Fossil evidence
3 Genetic evidence

4 Molecular evidence (DNA)
5 Evidence from proteins
6 Vestigial and atavistic organs
7 Embryology
8 Biogeography[113]
9 Homology[114]
10 Bacteriology, virology, immunology, pest-control

- The theory of evolution is demonstrable, testable, verifiable, peer-reviewed and falsifiable. It is agreed upon and has applications in almost every field of natural science.

- There are no valid alternatives to the theory of evolution at present, not is there likely to be. Creationism (or, Intelligent Design as it is sometimes known) is neither theory nor fact. It is, at best, only an opinion. It explains absolutely nothing, it is scientifically useless, and to only call it *wrong* would be giving it way too much credit.

- You will occasionally hear this pseudo-argument still being used: "If we came from monkeys, then why are there still monkeys?"

---

[113] Locations of species on the planet
[114] Similarities in structure between parts of different organisms, like the wing and the human arm, due to common ancestry.

My response to this usually starts with "If we came from dust, why is there still dust?", or "If Americans came from Britain, why are there still British people?" That is usually good enough to shut up the garden variety NASCAR fans[115], er, I mean Christians. For the astute theist, however, I may choose to begin my retort in roughly the following manner: Five or Six million years ago, an ape-like species roamed the rainforests of Africa. Over time, the rainforests began to be replaced with grasslands. The new environment favored those genetic traits which allowed the species to walk on two feet, work together as a team and use tools, all of which are useful against fast-moving predators. These eventually evolved into the modern homo sapiens. Not all of the early ape-like animals moved out of the dwindling forests, however. Those that remained were geographically separated from the rest of the species and evolved independently into modern great apes and old world monkeys, respectively. So no, we didn't "come from monkeys". We both evolved from a common ancestor who happened to look more

[115] I apologize for that gross over generalization. Not all NASCAR fan are are deluded Christians with below-normal intelligence. Case in point: My father. Huge NASCAR fan, extremely bright and not a Christian. His form of deism is loosely based on ancient native American animism, however, making it equally worthy of mockery and ridicule in my opinion (don't tell him I said that, he can still kick my ass).

like an ape than a human. Biology, genetics, homology and the *vast* fossil record confirms this. Evolution is a *fact*, this is not a debatable issue.

- "But why do we not see any transitional species?" Because you do not *want* to see any transitional species! I could refer you to a reputable scientific source such as the Talk Origins Archive (http://www.talkorigins.org/faqs/faq-transitional.html) which lists *hundreds* of examples of transitional species between fish and amphibians, amphibians to reptiles, reptiles to birds and reptiles to mammals, but you won't crack the book, open the website or read the evidence. Why? Because you'd rather stick your fingers in your ears and shout "lalalalalalala!".

- I'm going to admit something to you. It's supposed to be a secret. You are absolutely right! You figured us out. Tens of thousands of scientists have all conspired to invent the evidence, and we hid it from everyone! It's an awful lot of work, publishing fake papers, peer reviewing fabricated data. We hold secret meetings to plot it all out. We even have a secret☐ handshake! We've been doing it for 150 years. We do it for Satan, our lord and master, because we all hate God and want to sin. Busted!

Creationists: Please point to the precise pixel in this photo that is the "transitional species" between black and white.

$\mathcal{Y}$ou are trying to use your atheism and/or material possessions to fill a god-shaped hole in your heart.

- Christian logic:
1 Rich atheist - Probably attained his wealth using shady business practices. Spoiled trust fund baby. God allows him to be wealthy now because he is gracious and wants him to be happy in this life before his eternal torment in Hell.

2   Rich Christian - God has blessed him. It is his reward for living a Christian lifestyle. God has a mission for him to be a community leader.
3   Poor atheist - Lazy, lacks morality. Selfish and probably lives off the government system. Doesn't care about God, so he is reaping what he sows.
4   Poor Christian - How fortunate for him! He will be favored in Heaven.[116]

- How arrogant it is to walk up to a person you barely know, assert that you have identified their prime deficiency, and are confident that *you* have the solution.

- You will never hear me say "you have a big science-shaped hole in your brain that you fill with rationalizations about an invisible sky-wizard". Wait a second, as I wrote that last sentence, it rather occurred to me that it is *precisely* something I would say!

- If there is a hole in our hearts that is shaped like the *Christian* god, how do followers of other religions manage to fill it so well with *their* beliefs?

- We are mammals, we seek out love, comfort and acceptance. I am willing to give a little

---

[116] Matt. 20:16, 5:5, 19:24, 10:25; Luke 18:2, 6:24-25, Mark 10:25

ground and accept that belief in (somehow) living on after our death can may be quite comforting. That doesn't make it correct however. I would much rather *tentatively accept* an uncomfortable truth than *believe* a comfortable lie.

- Did you honestly seek out and fairly evaluate the happiness and contentment of non-religious people, or did you simply take a quick mental inventory of your preconceptions and then spout out the estimated outcome? Here's some research on the topic: Sweden, Denmark, France, Norway, Hong Kong, and Japan are in the top 10 of the world's least religious countries[117], and yet they are considered the most prosperous, happy, and have the world's highest living standards. Study after study indicates that the world's happiest countries are also the least religious.

- Perhaps you have a *god-shaped puppet hole* in your back!

- When I'm blue I sit back and think about my family and friends, what they mean to me, how much I love them, and how they enrich my life.

---

[117] On the question "is religion an important part of your daily life, only 14% to 27% of the population of these countries said "yes", Gallup Poll 2007-2008

I'm feeling better in no time. No god stuff, just human stuff.

I will pray for you.

- If given the choice, I would rather you not include me in your madness. If you feel you need to however, go ahead and invoke my name next time you kneel down, clasp your hands together and talk to the ceiling. It still won't change *anything*.

- You *pray* for me, and I'll *think* for both of us!

- Praying is begging. It's basically assuming that *you* are *so* important that you can ask your omniscient deity to change its already-made-up mind, and it will.

- "And I'll be sure to sacrifice a goat or a virgin[118] in your honor!"

- Praying to say thank you is actually arrogance dressed up as humility. You are saying "thank you for the blessings I have received", but what you're *really* saying is "thank you for putting *me* first and making *me* so wonderful/talented/rich/successful. Never mind the less fortunate who also pray."

- "Whatever keeps you off drugs."

- In *Christianese*, that is just a passive-aggressive, corrective, shaming and judgmental way of saying "you are wrong about being atheist and I will patronize you by letting you think that I feel sorry for you", and "it pisses me off that you are as happy as I am".

---

[118] Yahweh allowed Jephthah to sacrifice his virgin daughter in return for victory in battle (Judges 11:39)

- "Oh good. I was worried you were wasting your prayers on starving children or terminal cancer patients."

- Sure you could just *sit* there and feel like you're making a difference, but if I *needed* you, would you give me a phone call? Would you come visit me? Would you bring me soup if I got sick? Would you be a *friend* to me?

- Praying has always seemed to me like an exercise in self-gratification. When I hear "I will pray for you", it always comes out as "I will masturbate for you". It might make you feel better, but don't expect me to benefit from it.

- If the person who says this to you is already familiar with your religious position, they are often trying to impose their beliefs on you, or play the superiority card. As tempting as it is to just be polite and overlook their statement, this is sometimes your best opportunity to give them a piece of your mind.

What do you tell your children?
How do you raise your children?

- What do you mean by "raise" your children? It sounds as if you are implying that it is the job of parents is to indoctrinate children into a particular belief system. Do your offspring not have minds of their own? Would it not be the most prudent course of action to let them think for themselves, when they are old enough to do so?

- It is not beyond the capability of most parents to, in the most unbiased manner possible, teach their children what religion is and impart the tenets and beliefs of the major religions on earth. Then, let them make up their own minds as to which religion is right for them, or to choose no religion at all.

- My parents were Southern Baptists, but encouraged me to make up my own mind. I went to church with them on Sundays. I was even "saved" by a teenager in my driveway one morning. At the age of six, near the end of my second summer of "Vacation Bible School", my parents were politely asked that I not return next summer. The reason? "His questions are influencing the rest of the students." By age eight I was referring to myself as an "agnostic", and realized that I had been the "A-word" all along by high school ("atheist" or "asshole"? That remains to be seen!). I would like to think that I "was so created that I cannot not believe", but it is far more likely that it's just a case of good parenting, devoid of psychological indoctrination of any form.

Incidentally, Pastor Simmons and his assistant, whose name escapes me, both left the clergy shortly after that last summer of "VBS". Other factors were certainly the cause of their resignations, but I've always wondered if my incessant "tough questions" flipped a switch in their heads.

"The defining value of free thought is the right of individuals to think for themselves. Childhood indoctrination of any kind denies that right. Parents instill values, but choosing a worldview that expresses those values must be in the hands of the individual. Children should not be labeled in any way."[119]

- There is no such thing as a Catholic, Muslim or atheist child. Children are too young to know where they stand on this issue. Indoctrination at an early age is child abuse.

- "My daughter is a Republican", "his son is a Marxist", my kids are Libertarians just like me". See how ridiculous that sounds when applied to *political* affiliations?

[119] McGown, "Parenting Beyond Belief - On Raising Ethical, Caring Kids Without Religion"
119

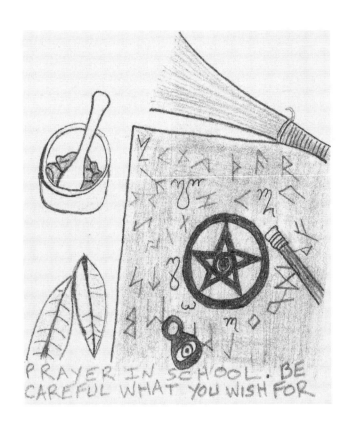

PRAYER IN SCHOOL. BE
CAREFUL WHAT YOU WISH FOR

Logical Fallacies

No counter-apologetics handbook would be complete without a list of commonly used fallacious arguments that you're bound to hear:

- Circular Reasoning: "God wrote the Bible. The Bible says God exists. Therefore, God must exist."
- Appeal to Majority: (See the Title of this book.)
- Appeal to Fear: "I love you too much to see you burn in Hell".
- Ridicule: "You're blind if you can't see that God exists. Why don't you just open your eyes and accept Jesus into your heart?"
- Flattery: "You're too intelligent to not believe in God."
- Straw Man: "Well Stalin, Hitler and Pol Pot were atheists."[120]
- Slippery Slope: "Taking prayer out of public schools is causing the downfall of our civilization".
- Moving the Goalpost: "We prayed that Grandpa wouldn't require open heart surgery. After the surgery, we were thankful that our prayers at least helped him through the successful procedure."

- Equivocation: "Atheists lack belief in God. Therefore, all atheists are certain that there is no God."

---

[120] Here I have to point out two things: 1.Hitler was not an atheist. 2.No dictator, to my knowledge, has *ever* committed an atrocity *in the name of atheism*. Compare that to atrocities committed in the name of Yahweh or Allah.

- Poisoning the Well: "You atheists are always trying to push your liberal gay rights agenda on everyone."
- Special Pleading: "Everything that exists had a creator. God exists, but he didn't require a creator because he has always existed."
- Appeal to Tradition: "Every human culture in history has had some type of religion. There must be truth to it."
- Post Hoc: "I prayed that you would make it home safely. You made it home safely. Therefore, my prayers were answered."
- Appeal to Faith: "Why would Yahweh send two bears to kill 42 children that were making fun of the prophet Elisha?" "Unless you have faith, you wouldn't understand".
- Wishful Thinking: "I couldn't live in a world where this is all there is. I believe that we will be given perfect bodies when we get to heaven and we will reunite with all our loved ones."
- Appeal to Personal Experience: "I was dead on the operating table for seven minutes and met God face to face."
- Burden of Proof: "You cannot prove God doesn't exist. Therefore, God exists."
- Affirming the Consequent: "If the Bible is the word of God, it would still be in existence today. The Bible is in existence today. Therefore, the Bible is the word of God."
- Bifurcation: "Either God created the universe or the universe came into existence from nothing.

The universe didn't come from nothing. Therefore, God created the universe."

- Argumentum Ad Nauseam: "There are no transitional fossils. There are no transitional fossils. There are no transitional fossils."
- Ipse Dixit: "If Christianity is good for the U.S. Presidents, it's good enough for me."
- Red Herring: "You may have hominid fossil specimens, but how did life get here in the first place?"
- Tu Quoque: "If atheists have such a higher standard of morality, why do you cuss, drink and drive over the speed limit?"
- Non Sequitur: "How do I know the universe was created in six days? Just look at those mountains and trees."

FALLACIOUS ARGUMENT BINGO
(Try It With Your Friends)

Special Pleading	Post Hoc	Poisoning the Well	Straw Man	Ad Hominem
Appeal to Authority	Slippery Slope	Ridicule	Circular Reasoning	Moving the Goalpost
Appeal to Majority	Flattery	Appeal to Fear	Equivocation	Wishful Thinking
Appeal to Faith	Appeal to Personal Experience	Burden of Proof	Affirming the Consequent	Bifurcation
Argumentum Ad Nauseam	Red Herring	Tu Quoque	Non Sequitur	Ipse Dixit